THE GROOM'S GUIDE

JAMES LOVE

THE
GROOM'S
GUIDE

JAMES LOVE

NEW HOLLAND

First published in 2007 by New Holland Publishers
London • Cape Town • Sydney • Auckland
www.newhollandpublishers.com

Garfield House, 86–88 Edgware Road, London, W2 2EA, United Kingdom
80 McKenzie Street, Cape Town, 8001, South Africa
14 Aquatic Drive, Frenchs Forest, NSW 2086, Australia
218 Lake Road, Northcote, Auckland, New Zealand

ISBN 978 1 84537 689 5

Although the publishers have made every effort to ensure that information contained in this
book was meticulously researched and correct at the time of going to press, they accept no responsibility
for any inaccuracies, loss, injury or inconvenience sustained by any person using this book as reference.

Publishing Manager: Jo Hemmings
Senior Editor: Steffanie Brown
Editor: Liz O' Donnell, Naomi Waters
Designer: Adam Morris
Production: Hema Gohil

Additional text by Naomi Waters

Cover reproduction by Pica Digital Pte Ltd, Singapore
Printed and bound in India by Replika Press PVT Ltd

10 9 8 7 6 5 4 3 2 1

CONTENTS

INTRODUCTION

If you are reading this book, then it means that you are engaged to be married – or at least seriously thinking about it – so, congratulations! You are embarking on a great journey. This book is designed to take you step-by-step through everything that will be happening between now and the big event.

The days when the groom simply had to turn up looking smart, give a speech and whisk his bride off on a honeymoon are long gone. Nowadays you are expected to get more involved in the details of planning your wedding. You will be asked by your fiancée to have an opinion on the relative merits of three different cake icings; to distinguish between ivory and off-white satin; to express a preference between various place-settings and cutlery designs.

The news agent's shelves are groaning under the weight of wedding magazines aimed at the bride-to-be, designed to help her make these decisions. And you can bet your life she'll be coming home laden with magazines, fabric and invitation samples and pretty wedding planners, and immersing herself in all things matrimonial.

But what about the groom? There is very little out there aimed at you. That's where this book comes in. Now don't worry, reading this book will not turn you into a professional flower arranger. But, among many other things, it will help you understand why apparently insignificant details can assume such importance.

Without wishing to stereotype you and your fiancée – this is the 21st century after all – it is probably a safe bet that she has already spent far more time dreaming about and visualising her wedding day than you have. Along the way, the details of the wedding may obscure the life-changing significance of what you are doing. I have lost count of the times a bewildered groom has come to me, after a tiff with his fiancée, telling me something like, "All I said was that I wasn't that bothered, she could choose what flowers we had on the tables, and she accused me of not caring and not wanting to marry her!"

Not seeming enthusiastic about your wedding may come across as not being enthusiastic about your marriage. And, if your otherwise perfect and delightful bride-to-be has an inexplicable taste for pink marzipan bunny rabbits to decorate your wedding cake, it is in your interests as well to get involved with all these details!

Planning your wedding should be a fun and enjoyable experience, a unique journey that you are sharing with your future wife. Do get involved, and do enjoy it!

Weddings are big business these days. Some experts put the cost of the average wedding at close to £15,000, and this figure is growing all the time. One of your many duties as groom-to-be will be not to lose sight of what it's all really about, and to make your fiancée feel like the special person you know she is. This book will help you navigate your way through the minefield of organising a modern-day wedding.

Before we go any further, I want to share a true story with you about a friend of mine. I have known Steve for over 10 years and he has always been a spontaneous type of guy, so it came as no surprise that after seeing his girlfriend for a year or so, he decided he wanted to get married. Steve was adamant he would arrange his wedding his way. He did not want any help – it would be easy.

The wedding day went without a hitch, speeches were slick and funny, the food and wine were sublime. Later during the day Steve began ribbing me in a satisfied, "told-you-so" type of way that everything had gone according to plan.

Forty-eight hours later, I finally got the call . . .

Steve had booked their Caribbean honeymoon based on some images he saw on the Internet. Upon arrival everything seemed fine. He and his new wife checked into their rooms, ordered room service and went to bed . . . In the morning they both put on their new swimwear and ventured to the pool area. They were met with a hot tub full of naked couples cavorting around. He had not read the small print – and had booked a swingers' resort.

It only took me an hour to get them booked into a new resort; but I think it took Steve a lot longer to get back into his bride's good books. 'Planning, planning and planning' is the moral to this story.

CHAPTER 1
THE PROPOSAL

Proposing to your girlfriend is probably one of the most nerve-wracking moments of your life, so try to plan the circumstances of your proposal in advance. You've probably been thinking about it for some time, so you don't want to let yourself down at the last moment. Even if you haven't hired an orchestra or whisked her off to Paris, even if it's a quiet dinner at home, show her that you have thought about it and how much it means to you. Remember: you may be nervous, but your girlfriend probably has no idea what is about to happen, so try to remain as calm and normal as possible.

ASKING FOR HER HAND

You want to get off on the right foot with both sides of the family, so being courteous and sensitive to their feelings may well avoid putting noses out of joint from the start, particularly if one or both sets of parents may end up footing the bill for your wedding day!

If you think that your decision to get engaged might come as a surprise to your parents, it is worth sounding out your intentions with them before going any further. It is customary for you, the man, to ask your girlfriend's father for her hand in marriage. Today, most men propose first and then, as a mark of respect, ask for permission, but this is not the correct way to do things.

Seeking permission may seem old-fashioned today, but it is a polite and respectful gesture. Why not ask your future father-in-law out for a drink at the pub or a bite to eat? He will probably know what you are about to ask and will appreciate the gesture.

9

TOP TIPS

- Don't discuss your plans with too many friends, in case they filter back to your girlfriend.
- Ask your girlfriend's father for permission to marry his daughter beforehand. (Ask her mother if it is not possible to ask the father.)
- Unless you feel confident about your girlfriend's taste – perhaps she has dropped hints, pointed things out in a jeweller's window! – most women would prefer to choose their own ring, given the choice.
- On bended knee . . . This is one of the few times that tradition rules. Yes, get down on one knee and ask for her hand in marriage.
- Be prepared to start talking weddings straightaway!
- Stamina is needed now; you are in for the long run-up to your wedding; but remember, this should be an enjoyable time!

THINK ABOUT THE DETAILS

Of course, it is the sincerity and feeling behind your proposal that counts. This is a special and, usually, private moment, so be prepared to let your guard down, express your feelings, and tell her why it is you want to marry her so much! However, some attention to the external details can help to make it all the more special for both you and your girlfriend. So, read on.

When?

This is the million-dollar question and one that really has no 'correct' answer. Only you will know if marriage is something you are ready for, and whether a proposal from you is something you feel reasonably confident that she too will welcome!

Once you have made your decision on when you are going to propose, stick to it and try to enjoy the moment. Obviously, you can't account for any last-minute interruptions, but do whatever you can to make the moment calm, special and memorable.

There are certain times that could make it more meaningful:
• around Christmas, Valentine's Day, Easter, etc. (but see page 12)
• at some special anniversary for you as a couple: when you first met, when you first said you loved her, the anniversary of a particularly special outing or holiday you have shared.

Where?

First of all, don't think that you have to plan some elaborate setting or hold out for that dream sunset, as the more complicated and contrived you make it, the more could go wrong! It is you, not the restaurant or venue, that should make the occasion special.

The location could be dictated by a favourite place or memorable occasion, such as where you first met or kissed: this will make the moment all the more poignant. Unlike wedding venues, which have to be licensed, you really can propose anywhere. Here are some suggestions:
• in a restaurant
• at Disneyland Paris or Alton Towers
• while hiking, fishing, or camping
• on a sailboat

- on an aeroplane
- at a sports event
- at a covered bridge
- on top of the Empire State Building or on the London Eye
- while walking on a beach

How?

Remember you only intend to propose once in your life, so make the most of it. And don't forget – just to add to the pressure – that how you propose will be recounted time after time as the 'Proposal Story' for years to come. Here are some ideas to get you thinking:
- down on one knee, anywhere
- hide a ring in a bouquet of flowers
- tie a ring to a kite string or fishing line
- hide a ring in a box of chocolates
- put an ad in a newspaper
- ask a DJ on the radio to ask for you
- use the letter cubes while playing a game of Scrabble
- design a crossword puzzle

TOP 10 MISTAKES WHEN PROPOSING
1. Don't allow other women to try on the ring

We are going to talk about engagement rings in greater detail a bit later in this chapter (see pages 13–16). I strongly advise you to think carefully about buying the ring in advance without your girlfriend's input. However, if you do decide to buy the ring before you propose, it's a good idea to get a second opinion. Ask the advice of your girlfriend's sister or best friend. If she hasn't already shared with her friend her thoughts about the sort of engagement ring she would like one day, this friend will at the very least have a pretty good idea about the style of jewellery she will like. Remember, just because she likes contemporary jewellery or metals for everyday wear, she may want something quite different in an engagement ring – something she will wear for the rest of her life.

This said, don't use your girlfriend's friends as guinea pigs. Make sure your girlfriend is the first person to see and wear her ring. Let her enjoy the fun of showing it off for the first time.

2. Letting the cat out of the bag

When you're finally ready to pop the question, don't spill the beans to too many people beforehand. Sharing the news with friends and family is something you should do together. Your girlfriend won't want to feel that you took her acceptance of your proposal for granted.

3. Proposing on a holiday or birthday

Do consider picking a day meaningful to your relationship, such as the anniversary of your first date. Your girlfriend wants this day to shine. But think twice about proposing on a holiday that can't be yours as a couple in the future, for example, Christmas, when in years to come you may well be surrounded by family and not have much privacy to commemorate the occasion.

4. Not asking permission

Come on, it's tradition, so not asking your future father-in-law for his permission will lose you brownie points. See page 9.

5. Playing hide-and-seek with the ring

Imagine this: you're about to propose to your girlfriend when she swallows the ring because you hid it in an ice-cream cone or cocktail. Romantic good, hospital bad.

6. Putting her off the scent

Minutes before the proposal, attempting to lead her on by convincing her that you've got a court appearance coming up or that you won't be ready for marriage for years is not the way to go. You may well have seen that episode from Friends where Chandler does this to Monica – to disastrous effect!

7. Not creating that special atmosphere
Do your research and you'll probably find that many venues are happy to create a special setting for your proposal. For example, many cinemas will schedule private screenings, restaurants can provide champagne toasts, etc.

8. Exhibiting suspicious behaviour
As proposal time approaches, make sure your behaviour remains consistent with how you normally act. Repeatedly checking your pockets to make sure the ring is still there and coming up with bizarre excuses for your whereabouts can be dead giveaways.

9. The nonchalant proposal
A sure-fire way to ruin any proposal is to start with any of the following statements: 'You win', 'We're not getting any younger', 'In spite of what my mother says', 'I have sowed my wild oats.'

10. Losing sight of what the proposal is all about
Your proposal will be perfect if it is honest, heartfelt and passionate.

THE ENGAGEMENT RING
A very good friend of mine, Lance James, who has been my jeweller since I met him 10 years ago, has by far the best advice for buying an engagement or wedding ring. Here are Lance's top tips for buying an engagement (or wedding) ring:

1. Find a good jeweller
This doesn't have to be the most expensive shop in town or indeed the cheapest, but should be one that you feel comfortable in. Find someone you feel you can trust to give you the right advice. Recommendations are always a good way to go. If you and your fiancée go to buy the ring together, she may well have ideas about certain jewellers or designers she would like to visit.

2. Decide on your budget

Before you start looking at rings, have a clear idea of what your budget is as well as what your girlfriend's expectations are. This will help your jeweller guide you to the rings in your price range. Tradition dictates that you pay for the ring, and (depending on sources) that it should cost either one or two month's of your salary. But don't feel tied to this. You may well find the perfect ring for less than this amount. And, don't forget, there will be many more opportunities for splashing out in the forthcoming months.

> ### TOP TIP
>
> 'When you wear a ring everyday, don't settle for an everyday ring'. This is excellent advice from jeweller Lance James. If you remember nothing else from this part of the chapter, please fix this rule in your mind.

3. Is the ring practical to wear?

This depends on your fiancée's activities and lifestyle. The higher the setting of the gemstone in the ring, the more likely it is that it will get caught in hair, snag on clothes, or get knocked about.

4. Will it withstand everyday wear and tear?

Your engagement ring must withstand the rigours of everyday life. Surprisingly, one of the worst places for jewellery is an office environment where a lot of paper is used. Paper is mildly abrasive and constant exposure could wear out your jewellery over the long term. If you are concerned about this it is worth considering platinum as platinum will outlast gold many times over.

5. Will it hold the gemstone(s) securely?

It's worth remembering that six claws are generally safer than four, a bezel setting is safer than a claw setting and the higher the setting the more likely the stone is to have movement.

6. Does it look great?

If your fiancée's eyes light up when she sees it and she is smiling like a Cheshire cat, it's a pretty safe bet that you have found 'The Ring'. If choosing together, although you are paying for it, she is the one who is going to wear it, so let her have the final choice.

THE ROCK

Diamonds are the traditional choice for an engagement ring and they go with everything. Unless you know that your girlfriend has a particular dislike for them or has an absolute love for another stone, then you cannot really go wrong with a diamond. There are four variables commonly known as the 'Four Cs' which will affect the price you pay for your diamond.

Carat

This is the unit measurement for a diamond. Each carat is made up of 100 points. However, do remember it is a measurement of weight and not the size. A diamond is a three-dimensional thing: a 1-carat diamond ring does not look twice the size of a 50-point diamond when viewed from above.

Colour

Most people want the whitest diamond they can afford. The colour is measured from D (colourless) down through the alphabet as the stone becomes more coloured. (The scale starts at D, because it cannot be ruled out that an even purer colour will be found in the future.) D and E are very expensive and extremely rare; most good-quality diamonds are between F and H.

Clarity

Because a diamond is a natural product, it will have natural imperfections ('inclusions'). The fewer inclusions, the more light is reflected from the stone, thus giving more sparkle.

Cut

The various different shapes of cut will affect the sparkle; the most effective cut is the brilliant or round cut. Your jeweller will be able to advise your further.

We all know that size does matter . . . but so does quality. All of the above information can be a little daunting and this is the reason that you must find a jeweller that you trust.

WEDDING RINGS

When choosing your wedding ring, remember it will become a symbol of all you will experience during your married life. It will last for much longer than the dress, be looked at more than the photos and will say, 'Hands off!' my husband (or wife). Your rings are the symbols of your love and commitment to each other, so take the time to choose rings that have a design that will last and that are of the highest quality achievable within your budget.

Start looking at the same time as choosing the other big things for your wedding, especially if you want a bespoke ring made or engraved. Choose a ring that is expressive of your style and personality. There is no wrong style of wedding ring.

Design

Most of us think that a wedding ring is just a plain band of gold, but there is so much more to wedding rings than that, with designers coming up with new colours, styles and designs all the time. Going for a classic timeless design doesn't necessarily mean you have to choose a plain wedding band. However, do try and imagine wearing your wedding ring in 20 years' time; look at the rings of people who have been married for 20 years, have they stood the test of time?

If your fiancée intends to wear her ring alongside her engagement ring, then you may need to consider a shaped band for her. It's worth remembering that different metals wear at different rates. Putting two different metals together will cause wear and tear on the softer metal.

It is not absolutely necessary for the wedding rings to match your fiancée's engagement ring. If she wants something different, try wearing them on different hands, as is done on the Continent.

Quality

Price will affect quality; a wedding ring has to last a lifetime. Spend as much as you can afford on your wedding bands. After all, you will be spending thousands on your wedding day, which lasts just 24 hours. The wedding rings are the only reminder you will wear every day from that day forwards.

Pay attention to the weight of the ring as looks can be deceptive. Lighter rings are less hardwearing and more difficult to repair. A smaller, more solid ring is better than a larger but lighter version.

Metal

If you wish to wear your ring gardening, doing DIY or rock-climbing, you should consider a harder-wearing material. Platinum is the hardest of all the precious metals, although there is a trend in alternative materials, including titanium and steel, which are both very resilient. The purer the gold, the softer it is – so 22 carat is the softest, 18 carat is in the middle and 9 carat is the hardest.

Size

Obviously, it is important to get the size right. Get it checked where you are buying the ring, so if it turns out to be too small or too large, it won't be down to you to pay for the repair. Not everyone gets this simple task right (and this can cause a major stress if it's two days before the wedding!). So go to a jeweller who knows their craft, not a just a shop that sells jewellery.

If you are not used to wearing rings, it is bound to feel strange. If it doesn't, this could mean it is too big. You don't want to lose it on your honeymoon, so get this checked out by your jeweller.

CHAPTER 2
THE ENGAGEMENT PARTY

So, you've proposed with style and aplomb, and been accepted. You've been out and bought an engagement ring. It's official, you are now engaged to be married! Every milestone in life deserves a celebration to mark the occasion, and your engagement is definitely one of them. This may well be the last big party you throw before you become man and wife, and it's a great opportunity for friends and family from both sides to get together and meet before the wedding itself. From now up until your wedding day you will need to keep organised, and planning an engagement party is a good place to start. It may even teach you a few useful lessons for planning the actual wedding.

ANNOUNCING YOUR ENGAGEMENT

Most girls go a bit gaga straight after being proposed to, so we can safely assume that both your and her close friends and family have been informed (probably with over-excited phone calls just after the proposal itself). But you will be keen to let a lot of other people know. This is usually done by telephone – or perhaps email nowadays – or you can simply let the family and social 'grapevines' do the work.

If the number of your family members and friends is particularly large, you may also wish to place an announcement in the local or national newspapers. If your fiancée's parents are hosting the forthcoming nuptials (paying for most of it, that is), it is customary for her father to be responsible for making and paying for these public announcements.

Before the wording of the announcement is submitted, make sure that your parents have also been shown it for approval. This will help to make them feel included in these early stages. This maxim applies equally to planning the engagement party itself – make sure both sets of parents are consulted.

THE PURPOSE OF THE PARTY

Beyond having a jolly good time, that is!

An engagement party with close friends and family is particularly important for brides with a one-year-or-longer engagement. Although you are not yet actually married, you have entered a new phase of your relationship and commitment to each other. The main purpose of the event is to celebrate this commitment with those who are closest to you.

Secondly it celebrates the prospective union of your two families. It is a great opportunity for everyone in your bridal party to meet each other if they have not already done so. Once both sets of future in-laws have met, discussions can commence on the forthcoming nuptials. These days, as most couple's parents will already have met, it is a jolly good reason to overindulge!

WHO HOSTS THE PARTY?

There are no real set rules today for who should host the engagement party. However, if you are following tradition, then the party should be hosted by the parents of the bride.

WHAT STYLE OF PARTY?

The formality of the event can range from a simple barbecue to a sit-down dinner or a full-blown banquet at a castle. The style and dress code of your party depends on what the bridal party decides.

Springing a surprise party is better left for birthdays and anniversaries. This is an occasion when your fiancée will want to look her best to show off her engagement ring and she can't do that if she has just got back from shopping in her tracksuit. Trust me, this is a no-no.

TOP TIP

Planning your engagement party is really no different from organising any other type of party, so don't get unduly stressed about it. But this is one party you intend to throw only once in your lifetime, so remember to enjoy it!

More and more couples these days throw more than one engagement 'party'. Don't be alarmed, this could actually make things simpler. It can help accommodate different age ranges and make travel arrangements for guests easier. For example, you may have a more formal dinner or garden party hosted at your fiancée's family home, for both the immediate families only. This is a particularly good idea if the families do not yet know each other well. Not having too many other friends around will mean that you can focus on helping everyone to get along, and create that special family atmosphere. Have no illusions; your engagement represents the union of two families, not just two people.

Then, you and your fiancée may decide to have a more informal get-together at your own home, or perhaps in a restaurant, for your friends, colleagues and usual social crowd. This means that you and your fiancée need not be on your 'best behaviour' *quite* so much, and can let your hair down a bit more. I think I can safely assume that you and your girlfriend have thrown parties or booked a restaurant before, so the following advice applies to the bigger, slightly more formal affair!

WHEN?

The engagement party is usually held a few months after your proposal (believe me, it will take you that long to get things organised) and about one year before your chosen wedding date. You do not have to throw your engagement party on the day of the announcement.

Evening or weekend events are usually the better option. A weekend garden party or a barbecue are ideal if the weather permits.

Make sure that all the key people are available before booking a caterer or sending out invites. It's no good having a party when the bride's parents are away on a cruise in the Caribbean.

WHO SHOULD WE INVITE?

Who is on your guest list is entirely up to you and your fiancée. It can be just you, the couple, and both sets of parents, or pretty much everyone who will be invited to the wedding. This means you could have more than 100 guests.

TOP TIP

When planning your party, it is only right to remember that most of the people attending the party will probably expect to be invited to the wedding itself, so choose your guest list wisely. The last thing you want is to bump into that old friend or second cousin and have them ask you when you're getting married – three months after you've returned from your honeymoon.

Usually, written invitations are sent out, but in the age of the Internet, e-mail is becoming a great way to get fast replies. If you are having a small gathering, verbal communication may be all that you need. However you invite your guests, be sure to include an RSVP with a contact e-mail address and telephone number.

THE PARTY VENUE

This is totally down to the type of event that you and your fiancée have decided to have. Generally, most engagement parties take place at one of the homes of either set of parents, but should you wish to hold it at your home that's fine too. Planning an event at a restaurant or venue can be costly, but might be ideal for a smaller or less formal gathering. If you do go down this route then make sure that one person/set of parents assumes overall control, to prevent any confusion or crossed wires.

FEEDING AND WATERING YOUR GUESTS

Your menu can be anything from simple appetisers to a traditional home-cooked meal, buffet or barbecue. Even when planning your party at home, it can be a good idea to hire outside caterers. This leaves you and your fiancée time to meet all your guests and to enjoy the event without having to worry about getting the canapés out of the oven or running out of drinks.

ENGAGEMENT PARTY ETIQUETTE

Don't expect gifts at engagement parties. Stating this on the invites will also clarify the issue for your guests. Some guests may still want to bring a gift, even if they are not expected to. If this does happen, wait until after the party to open them in order not to embarrass guests that have not brought you a gift. Make sure that you send a thank-you note to all guests who do bring you a gift.

Don't feel compelled to make a toast at your party. However, if some of your guests and family want to propose a toast, then that is fine, and there is no need to have this pre-planned – the bride's father will probably pick a suitable moment.

Are you planning entertainment? If so, make sure that you get written confirmation from the singer/band/DJ at least two weeks before your party.

Another great idea is to have a guest book for your guests to leave messages and good wishes.

ENGAGEMENT PARTY CHECKLIST
3 months before
Set your date and venue. Remember, this is not the actual wedding, so show restraint on the budget. Discuss and compile the guest list. Research and book a caterer, if you are having one.

1 month before
Send out invites and make sure your guests RSVP. Buy any accessories that you need, such as balloons, etc. Create a list of food and drink if you are doing the catering yourself.

2 weeks to 1 day before
Buy all non-fresh party items such as alcohol, soft drinks and paper plates. Arrange for glasses to be picked up (some supermarkets offer a free glass-rental service).

The day before
Put away any breakable items in your home. Check that your suit and your shoes are clean (very important!). Decorate the house if you are doing so. Buy the fresh food items and start to prepare it.

On the day
Make sure that you have somewhere to store coats, etc. Put out all food and drink. Put someone in charge of offering drinks to guests as they arrive. Place bins around the house so that your guests can dispose of their paper plates and empty bottles. Most of all, enjoy the beginning of your engagement and wedding plans.

CHAPTER 3

THE GROOM'S ROLE

It is not unusual for a groom to feel more than a little left out of the planning stages of the wedding. It can seem that you, the groom, had the most important duty to perform in proposing, but now all eyes are focused on your fiancée. Obviously, your presence on the actual day is just as vital to the occasion as hers, but there is plenty that you must – and can – be doing between now and then. This chapter gives an overview of all your responsibilities, which are then explored in greater detail in the following chapters.

As the groom, you naturally have some very important responsibilities in order for your wedding to run smoothly. I am sure the first one that springs to mind is getting completely hammered on the stag do, but alas this is at the bottom of the list.

WHO DOES WHAT?

Tradition dictates that some tasks are your responsibility, some are a joint responsibility between you and the bride, and others are the bride's father's – if he is bearing the bulk of the cost. Who *does* what therefore depends to some degree on who is *paying* for what, and the traditional breakdown of who pays for different elements of the wedding are set out fully in Chapter 4 (pages 34–36) and at the back of this book (pages 112–113). However, here is an overview of the main things you are traditionally expected to organise.

RESPONSIBILITIES OF THE GROOM
Buying the engagement ring

Some grooms present their fiancée with the ring at the time of proposing, but most brides, given the chance, would prefer to choose their own. See Chapter 1.

Handling the paperwork

– to do with the Registration of your marriage, the marriage certificate, and paying fees for the church or Registrar.

Choosing your best man and ushers

– and making sure they know what their duties are. More about this in Chapter 7.

Booking the honeymoon

Tradition states that the groom arranges this as a surprise for his bride, but you may decide to do this together. While traditionally the groom pays for the honeymoon, it is now common to make it part of the overall wedding budget. If you're going on a long-haul trip, make sure that you have all necessary inoculations. You will need to order any traveller's cheques and foreign currency, and make sure you have all passports (hers as well as yours) and necessary travel documents in a safe and accessible place on the day. See Chapter 11.

Organising your wedding-day transport

It is very important to make sure that you actually see the cars and, where possible, have a short run in them. You want the peace of mind that they will actually get you to the church on time. So make sure you, your best man, and the drivers know the exact route you will be taking. Nearer the time, it might be worth checking that there are not any roadworks or diversions along your intended route!

Choosing outfits

– for your self, your best man and your ushers. Most grooms rent their suits, and there are some fantastic designs and styles in many high-street stores. Companies such as Moss Bros have over 100 stores nationwide and will help you choose the best style, design and colour for your wedding. It will be up to you – or you could delegate the task to your best man – to collect the outfits for you, your best man and the ushers. See Chapter 7 for more advice about what to wear.

Booking the bridal suite

Now is not the time to be frugal. It's definitely worth splashing out as much as you can afford; it is, after all, your first night together as man and wife. Some venues will offer a room as part of the package, which can be a real boon if you or your bride have had a few too many glasses of champagne or worn your feet out on the dance floor: no need to get changed and drive somewhere else – just troop upstairs to the bridal suite! Alternatively, you may want to get away somewhere different for your first night as husband and wife.

Your speech

Chapter 10 is devoted solely to helping you create a cracking speech, and you'll find some sample speeches and appropriate quotes to use at the back of the book.

Enjoying a fantastic stag night!

Having it a month before the wedding will ensure that you not only make it to the church on time but also that you will be in a fit state to enjoy your big day. Again, it's an important occasion, so this book has devoted the whole of Chapter 8 to the Stag Do.

Personal grooming

Obviously it is up to you to take care of your own grooming arrangements: getting a hair cut about a week before the wedding day, and perhaps a manicure, so your hands are presentable when exchanging rings and in photographs.

Paying for things!

Some duties may not involve you actually *doing* an awful lot, but there are specific items for which you are expected to pay, for example: the bride's engagement and wedding rings; the church/Registrar's fee; the marriage certificate; the first-night accommodation; all going away transport; the honeymoon; gifts for the best man and ushers; a gift to your bride.

THINGS TO DO TOGETHER

These items will be expanded on in subsequent chapters, but in brief:
• Deciding on the type of wedding you want: large or small; religious or civil; traditional or modern; at home or abroad.
• Working out your total wedding budget with your fiancée – and, most likely, with both your families as well – and deciding how you will allocate your cash.
• Setting the date of the wedding.

• Choosing and booking your venue(s).
• Choosing your wedding rings.
• Choosing gifts for the best man, ushers and bridesmaids.
• Perhaps taking dancing lessons for your first dance on the day?
• Choosing the style of your invitations and other wedding stationery.
• Drawing up a seating plan for your guests.
• Compiling a gift list, if you are having one.
• Choosing a photographer and videographer.
• Choosing a caterer and menu.

ON THE DAY

Again, covering everything you will need to do on this biggest of days is a chapter in itself – see Chapter 9.

BEING SUPPORTIVE

I am often asked 'What's the single most important thing that I can do to help the wedding go smoothly?'. Perhaps an even better question to ask is, 'What can I do to make the engagement/planning go smoothly?' If I had to choose one bit of advice over all others, it would be to be there for your fiancée, be her rock, because God knows that with all the detailed planning and anxiety about how she's going to look on the big day, she will need someone who is going to be completely understanding, caring and loving – in short, the person who she agreed to marry.

True story

While Steve's fiancée was out choosing her wedding dress, she called him at work. Her voice had a somewhat urgent tone, and she proceeded to ask him if he preferred white, eggshell or ivory. Now Steve has always considered himself something of a thinker, and eggshell and ivory were 'white' as far as he was concerned, so he replied with some conviction, 'eggshell'. After a short pause, his fiancée sweetly thanked him for his opinion and said she was going for ivory.

One of the key responsibilities of the groom throughout all stages of planning the wedding is to make sure that when all around him are losing their minds, he stays focused and level-headed. Giving your fiancée peace of mind is paramount, as most brides will at some time during the build-up get a bit emotional or upset. It is at this point that you will need to be her rock.

Every now and again it is healthy and, quite frankly, necessary to just forget about the wedding and get away from it all. It will probably be up to you to spot when this is needed. Here are a few ideas to help keep even the most demanding bride happy and sane.

• Have a picnic (weather permitting). This is a great romantic way to relax and spend an afternoon.

• Take a drive, maybe into the country or somewhere you both love to visit and have lunch in a secluded restaurant or country pub.

• Treat yourselves to a weekend away, perhaps to a romantic European city. With all the no-frills airlines, it's not too expensive.

• A special meal. Make your fiancée a candle-lit dinner with all the trimmings. Be sure not to forget a small box of chocolate truffles, a nice bottle of wine and maybe a chick flick for afterwards.

• Go to the seaside. This never fails to relax and invigorate.

• Pamper night. When your fiancée comes in from work have a hot bubble bath run with candles and a glass of wine or champagne. . .

These are just a few ideas to lighten the inevitable stress of the many months of planning that you and your bride will go through, but whatever trials and tribulations you suffer over the coming months, remember that this is all about the two of you getting married and spending the rest of your lives together.

CHAPTER 4

PLANNING

Now it's time to get stuck into the nitty-gritty of planning your wedding. It can seem overwhelming – and far more complicated than you ever imagined. There are so many components required, so many different people needed in order for it to be the day you dreamed of. From budgeting, choosing ceremony and reception venues and booking entertainment and photographers, to choosing a menu and arranging the wedding-day transport, there is a lot for you to do! Knowing your priorities and delegating certain tasks to others will help you get there unscathed.

EXPECTATIONS

It is a pretty safe bet that most brides-to-be have a very good idea of what they expect from their wedding day even before they know they are getting married. Now, obviously, as men of the 21st century, we all understand that it is imperative that what the bride wants the bride gets, and we will do everything in our power to make sure that she gets her dream wedding.

But while the bride usually has a clear mental picture of how she wants her wedding day to unfold, it is rare for the groom to have any firm or preconceived ideas about it. Most men are brought up believing that the wedding day is all about the bride – that all eyes will be on her. But this is rapidly changing. When asked, over 75 per cent of all brides said that they would like more input from their fiancés when planning their wedding, believing it would make the planning process more romantic, and the actual day more meaningful, if they knew their husband had been actively involved.

It is important to discuss both your and your bride's expectations of the wedding early on. Come up with a list of the key features and all your ideas and split the list into three main sections.

Essentials

Non-negotiable. This is a list of everything that you both definitely want at the wedding and under no circumstances will you compromise on them. Perhaps you both know you want a church wedding, a small wedding, or a wedding overseas.

Possibles

Negotiable. These are the ideas that one or both of you weren't entirely convinced about. Perhaps one of you wants to write your own vows, and the other one is not so keen. Perhaps one of you wants to break with tradition in the clothes you wear, while the other has not considered this possibility. This list is about being creative: expanding and compromising on these ideas until you both agree on them or discount them completely.

Off the wall!

Here you put down anything that you both agreed was a bit 'out there'. It could be a dream that the bride has had since she was a child about a particular theme for the whole wedding. Perhaps you want to arrive at the church in a Second World War tank, or get married during a parachute jump. Now, I'm not saying for one moment that you take everything in this section seriously; however, you never really know when something a little bit wacky will take shape into a fantastic idea.

How much time do you need for planning?

If you want to get married quickly, say within a few months or so, then it is advisable to hire a professional wedding planner. If your wedding date is around eight months or more in the future, you will have ample time to plan your wedding. The rule is: make the time.

SETTING THE DATE

Friends and family keep asking you 'When's the big day?'. You've now both had a little time for the whole wedding idea to sink in. Well, as with most things, nothing is as simple as you might think. You can't just pick a date out of thin air as there are too many variables that ride on the date that you pick.

The most common reason for a date being chosen is whether a particular venue has that date available, and with some venues booked up as far as two years in advance, you can see why.

If you are keen on a certain venue, check their available date or dates as soon as you can. Don't forget you will have to settle for a date that both the church/ceremony venue *and* the reception venue have free. Once you have booked your venues, then you are able to announce your wedding date.

Have you considered...?

There are many other factors to take into account – besides the availability of your venue – when setting the date of your wedding:

- Have any of the key people in the wedding party booked holidays that clash with that date?
- Are there any religious holidays that would cause restrictions?
- Have you absolutely set your heart on having your wedding at a particular time of year? The summer months are always the most popular, and thus tend to get booked up further in advance.
- Are there any other weddings of friends and family on that date?
- Are there any major sporting events that will mean some guests will already have prior engagements? If you and many of your friends are football mad, you don't want to be getting married on the day of the FA Cup final. Your bride won't appreciate you, the best man and all the ushers disappearing to watch the match!
- Have any of your close family or friends already booked holidays that cannot be altered? Your wedding could be a thin affair if your family are all away on holiday.
- Is the date during the school holidays? This could make it easier – or more difficult! – for some of your guests to attend. It can also mean that you will need to invite these children to the wedding, and provide certain facilities or entertainment for them.
- Check the weather. We all know that the weather cannot be predicted precisely. A winter wedding *can* be beautiful – if it's a bright, clear crisp day, with a sprinkling of snow on the ground. But how often can you count on that? You can check online what the previous few years' weather has been like and make a decision from there. Log on to www.theweddingnetwork.co.uk to check the weather record for your prospective date.
- Is the time of year you want to get married a good time to visit

TOP TIP

Save money on your wedding venue by avoiding Saturdays. Some venues give a discount of up to 50 per cent for couples getting married on either a Friday or Sunday. And perhaps you can take advantage of a Bank Holiday, as these make Sunday a prime day for a wedding as well.

your honeymoon destination? Our summertime is off season in the Caribbean, which is great for prices but not so good for sunshine.

Once your wedding date has been set, you can focus all your efforts on planning a fantastic day.

THE BUDGET

We would all like to have limitless resources for our wedding and honeymoon, but unfortunately most of us have to live in the real world and operate within a budget. This means working out exactly what you can afford to spend and sticking to it. Whatever amount you set as your budget, try to have a contingency fund for any extras or last-minute expenses.

Prioritising your budget is a great way to apportion funds. It works like this: make a list of items that you need to book/buy for your wedding according to how important each one is. The higher up the list, the less likely you are to want to compromise on price or quality. Conversely, there may be other items that you are not so concerned about, or end up not having altogether – and thus you can 'borrow' money from this item to boost the budget for your priority items.

This said, there is a usual price range that you can expect to pay for certain key things. The Wedding Network website has a budget planner facility which, if you type in your overall budget, will break it down and allocate it to all the different items for you.

Who is paying for it all?

Tradition states that the bride's parents pay for the bulk of the wedding. But one can't make assumptions these days. Be tactful when finding out how much they can afford, and grateful for any contribution. Nearly all couples now make some contribution to the cost of their wedding, if not paying for it in its entirety.

If your parents are paying the bill, or a substantial part of it, it is only reasonable that they will expect to have some sort of say in how that money is spent. Remember, traditionally speaking, the bride's parents are the 'hosts' of the event, and thus they will want to feel that overall it is done in a style they are comfortable with too.

Some sensitive negotiation may be necessary here, especially if they have 100 people in mind who they want to attend, but you wanted to have a small wedding, or vice versa. Whether you and your fiancée are paying, or everyone's chipping in, sensitivity is still necessary – but it *is* your wedding in the end.

Traditionally who pays for what? With so many religions and cultures in Britain today, it is difficult to create a definitive list. And, as previously stated, you and your bride may actually be paying for some, or all of this yourself. The following are some general pointers. (See also the Budget Planner on pages 112-113.)

Family of the bride (and/or the bride herself) pays for:
- Announcements
- Engagement party
- Bride's wedding dress, shoes and accessories
- Invitations, stationery and postage
- Choir/music
- The reception (including the wedding cake, caterers, food and drink, venue/marquee and entertainment)
- Flowers, decorations and accessories for ceremony and reception
- Photographer and videographer
- Gifts for the bride's attendants
- The seating-plan chart (if done professionally)
- Car hire for the bridal party on wedding day
- All tips for all services, e.g., parking, security

Family of the groom (and/or the groom himself) pays for:
- The bride's rings, including the engagement ring
- Church or Registrar's fee
- The marriage certificate
- Groom's suit and accessories
- All bouquets and buttonholes

- First-night accommodation
- All suits and accessories for the best man
- Gifts for the best man and ushers
- The honeymoon and travel

What can you afford?

Once you've set your budget, be realistic. Most venues work on a 'cost per head' basis. How many people can you afford to invite? Is it more important to you both to have everyone there, but a cheaper venue, with budget food? Or to pamper a smaller amount of people with a really elegant meal? If you're on a tight budget, you may just have to limit your numbers.

Don't waste money

The wedding industry is just that, an industry. While there are plenty of people giving good advice, there are also those who only want to profit from it. If you troop round a wedding show with your fiancée you will be overwhelmed at all the paraphernalia on offer – a bride could easily get carried away! Ask yourself, will this 'little extra' really make a difference to us and our guests on the day? Don't spend where you don't have to, whether it's your bride being seduced by an ultra-expensive wedding dress, or booking too many wedding cars. That said, while it may be hard to justify spending a small fortune on a dress that will be worn only once, the dress may be one of the most important things to the bride-to-be.

Don't forget the meaning of 'budget'

So everything started off well. But before you know it, you have spent twice the amount on the venue alone, and the only thing entertaining you is the exorbitant quote for your hired disco. Many couples would now just ditch the budget and end up starting married life saddled with an enormous debt. Don't.

Know your budget, and what's important to you both. Your bride does not want to walk up the aisle wishing she'd gone for the dress

TOP TIPS

If your budget does start to spiral out of control – or you simply need to keep costs down from the beginning – here are some money-saving tips:

- Get married on a weekday, when venues will be cheaper than at weekends.
- Make your own invitations.
- Serve Cava (Brut) not champagne. After a couple of glasses, they won't notice the difference.
- Ask a friend to do the wedding-day video, rather than paying a professional.
- Buffets are cheaper than sit-down meals.
- Don't have favours. They often get ignored or thrown away.
- Have fewer bridesmaids and ushers.
- Does a family friend have a classic or vintage car they would let you use?
- Instead of having a separate dessert course, serve your wedding cake as the dessert.

that cost 'merely' £200 more. You don't want to be sitting at the reception realising you never needed a seven-course meal.

Budgeting will not only help you afford your wedding, it's also a great skill to have for married life. Use the budgeting tools on www.theweddingnetwork.co.uk to help keep you in check.

Is wedding insurance necessary?

More and more couples are taking out wedding insurance to protect the investment they are making with their wedding day. With weddings costing upwards of £15,000, should one of the bridal party become ill or, God forbid, suffer an accident that stops them attending the wedding, insurance will give you the option to change your wedding date without worrying about the money. You can also insure against damage to the wedding photos, for instance, so, depending on the costs involved, wedding insurance is a good idea.

YOUR KEY ORGANISERS

A few key people are essential to the success of your special day, so it is important that you develop a good rapport with them.

The celebrant of the ceremony

This is the priest, vicar, minister, Registrar or other official who will be conducting the wedding ceremony, religious or civil. For those couples already practising a faith this may be of particular importance. They will be able to advise you on all procedures, possible readings, music and hymns.

If it will be a mixed-faith marriage, the ministers from both faiths will need to liaise with each other – and with you – as to what the ceremony will comprise of, and how it will be conducted.

Some faiths require marriage-preparation classes or, at least, attendance for some months at the relevant church.

The event organiser

There should be someone at your chosen reception venue to co-ordinate all your booking and wedding-day needs. This may be the owner, or a specific events/wedding coordinator. It's important that you feel comfortable with them, and that they show they are willing to listen to what you want and to cater to your needs. They should be available to you during the build-up to your wedding as well as on the day itself. You need to feel confident that, on the day, any of your guests could go to them and be helped appropriately.

The toastmaster, or master of ceremonies

This is the person responsible for keeping your wedding reception on track and on schedule (don't forget, a schedule on the day is important if your food is not to be served burnt or cold!), making sure the speeches happen at the correct time and announcing your first dance, etc. Many couples these days decide to forego a toastmaster, and these duties devolve to the best man.

The DJ or other entertainment

Your DJ must be kept informed of the type of music you want at the reception. You may also decide to have musicians at the church, a live band at the reception, and perhaps a children's entertainer.

CHOOSING A VENUE
The ceremony

You can have two types of wedding ceremonies: civil or religious. Although it will not take up the majority of the time – or budget – of your wedding day, it is this ceremony that makes you *married*. So take the time to ensure that it is just what you want. Many couples forget important things such as flowers in the ceremony venue, special music, readings and, most important of all, their vows.

More couples are opting for civil ceremonies over a traditional church wedding than ever before, due to a relaxation of the laws governing who can perform the wedding ceremony and where it can take place. You can now get married nearly anywhere that you want, providing that a licence is granted for that venue.

A civil ceremony is a non-religious legal marriage ceremony normally conducted by a Registrar. It cannot include hymns, religious readings or prayers. The marriage must take place at a registered or licensed venue to be legally valid in England and Wales. There are thousands of registered wedding venues across the UK, ranging from hotels and restaurants to stately homes. Some really unique places – the London Eye and even most football clubs – are also now licensed to conduct wedding ceremonies. You must first visit your local Register Office where they will explain how to register for your wedding and the fees that are payable.

For those wanting to get married in a church or other place of worship, first make an appointment to see your religious minister and discuss your plans. Some faiths will require you and your fiancée to attend church for a period of time, or to attend marriage-preparation classes, so make this appointment an early priority.

The reception

Weddings are big business and the most popular venues are booked up for years ahead (especially for the peak weekends between May and September). Once you have set your budget, start visiting possible venues and see which ones have the dates available that you are after. There are some important questions to ask to make sure that it really is suitable for the sort of reception you want:

• Do you like the menu on offer? Can you sample it beforehand? What is the price per head?

• What/how much alcohol does this package include?

• Can the venue cater for the number of guests you want to invite?

• Do they have a wedding coordinator on hand during the day?

• Is the reception venue within a reasonable distance of the ceremony? Is it easy to find, or well signposted?

• Are there restrictions on what time your reception has to finish?

• Is there any accommodation there, or nearby, for guests?

• Will you have the venue all to yourself? If not, which parts are going to be communal, free for other guests of the venue to access? This can spoil the sense of occasion – strangers walking through the midst of your photographs in order to find the lavatories. Or perhaps joining in the whole party and blagging free drinks!

• Are there adequate cloakroom and lavatory facilities?

• Are there facilities for less mobile or disabled guests?

• Are there any special facilities for children? Is there a room that a mobile crèche service could use?

• Are there sufficient car-parking arrangements?

• What decorations are included, such as balloons, flowers, table decorations, chair hire or covers?

If your queries have been answered to your satisfaction, then book the venue and get on with the rest of your planning duties.

CATERING

There's more to think about here than first meets the eye!

• You will need to make breakfast/brunch plans for you and the groom's party. So will the bride.

• Think about the time-scale of the day. A common complaint from guests can be that they spend too long waiting around for food! Take into account that your guests may already have travelled for some hours before the ceremony. How long will it be before they get some nourishment? Do you thus need to offer nibbles and refreshments immediately upon arrival at the reception venue?

• Do you want a sit-down meal, served by waiting staff? Or a buffet? Both have their merits. Be advised by your venue coordinator.

• Are you inviting children to your wedding? Will they need a special kiddies menu? Perhaps older children can be seated at their own table(s). This will help them to mix and have fun at what is, after all, a fairly adult affair. It may also enable their parents to enjoy themselves without having to worry about their offspring.

The wedding cake

Despite the bad taste (literally, and figuratively!) it can illicit, a wedding cake is an enduring tradition. Most couples getting married these days no longer want the all-white, collonaded, plaster-of-paris, figurine-topped construction! But there are many contemporary and modern alternatives, designed with a 21st-century couple in mind, and not a cupid or statuette in sight. Chocolate cakes are fast becoming the most popular style of cakes in the UK. Bakers can do just about anything these days. Your wedding cake can become the centrepiece of the wedding reception.

Feeding the 'hired help'

It's difficult to work efficiently on an empty stomach, whether you're the photographer or a member of the string quartet. So it is a good idea to include in your budget a few extra meals for any key organiser/contributor who is spending a large amount of time at the venue. There is no need to serve them at the same tables as your wedding guests, so ask your wedding coordinator to arrange a separate table for them. You will get far more out of your photographer if he or she is not starving.

Vegetarian and special dietary needs

Most venues will always have a vegetarian option on their menu, and should be able to accommodate other dietary needs.

Do you have to have champagne?

You are not obliged to serve champagne. If you are cutting out the bubbly because neither you nor your fiancée like the stuff, then simply fill your own glasses with your favourite poison and save the champagne for your guests. If you are looking to reduce the cost of your alcohol bill, then serve a Spanish cava (must be brut), which is usually a third of the cost. Or why not have the waiters hand out exotic cocktails, signature martinis or white-wine spritzers?

STATIONERY, FLOWERS AND DECORATIONS

Okay, despite it being the 21st century and all that, this is still probably much more the bride's domain than yours. She will probably want all this stuff coordinated along a certain theme, whether it be colour, season or style. Keep a hand in here, to make sure you're happy with it too.

ENTERTAINMENT

What sort of atmosphere do you want at your reception? The music – along with the venue – will go a long way to creating this.

• What, if any, music are you going to have at the ceremony?

• How long is your reception going to last? If some die-hards are going to dance on through till morning, then they may have been there for a good eight hours or more. Thus you will want a variety of music, which will cater to all tastes and age-groups.

• If you go for a DJ, then make sure he is someone who will really pay attention to your playlist of favourite songs, and that he is happy to take requests.

• Perhaps the entertainment is an area in which to show inventiveness! Hire a magician to go around the tables performing conjuring tricks? Or a troupe of professional salsa or tango dancers (with band included) who can give a cabaret performance and then will dance with your guests? Or a Ceilidgh band, with caller, to get everyone involved in big group dances?

• And what about the kids? If you are inviting children to your wedding – perhaps you both have lots of nephews and nieces – then it may well be worth considering hiring a couple of crèche staff or a children's entertainer to keep them occupied. Consider providing goody bags of toys and activities for each child. You may need to check safety arrangements with your venue coordinator.

TRANSPORT

Transport needs to be provided to take the bride to the ceremony venue, usually accompanied by her father, or whoever is giving her away. This will be the vehicle in which you and your new wife depart from the ceremony to go to the reception venue. It's a nice idea to arrange for a bottle of champagne and glasses to be on ice in the car so that you can have a celebratory toast as a married couple.

• Who else do you need to provide transport for? This should be moderated by the size of your budget, as booking eight separate cars can get expensive. How are you and your best man getting to the ceremony venue? It can be a nerve-wracking time, so it is worth booking something special for yourself too.

• What about the bridesmaids? The ushers? The mother of the bride? If you can't afford cars for all these different parties, and they don't have their own transport, at least pre-arrange lifts for them, perhaps from other family members.

• Who says you have to travel in cars? A horse-drawn carriage is particularly picturesque for a country wedding, though not practical for a long journey, or in mid-winter. Arriving at your reception in a helicopter can be great fun. Use your imagination, but be sensible too. Perhaps a 'character' car is the way to go: a pink cadillac or London taxicab?

• What about all your guests? Many weddings these days involve travelling some distance and at least one-overnight stay in a hotel or B&B. Perhaps you can lay on mini-bus transport or taxis to help ferry guests between hotels, venues or train stations. It might be an idea to nominate an usher to be on the look-out to help anyone needing a lift on the day.

PHOTOGRAPHY AND VIDEOS

Remember, these should last a lifetime and may be seen for generations to come. Think about the style of photography you want. There is the traditional sort, with all the various groups of relatives, or a more informal 'reportage' style. These can be wonderfully evocative and individual. Perhaps you want a mixture of both styles, and perhaps a mixture of colour and black-and-white. The best way to choose your photographer is to see examples of their previous work. This applies to the videographer too. If you're really splashing out on first-rate photographs, perhaps there is an obliging uncle who you can ask to do a fun video extra.

Many couples these days leave instant disposable cameras on the reception tables, for their guests to snap away with. Leave a box for the guests to deposit these in as they leave – or make sure they are collected up from the tables – so that you can then get them developed. The results can be most entertaining!

DELEGATING RESPONSIBILITIES

Having read this far, you are probably exhausted just thinking about everything that needs to be done! Here is a rough breakdown of suppliers that you need to book.

For the bride
All her bridal wear and accessories
Hair and beauty
Flowers – bouquets, buttonholes, church and venue flowers
Choosing bridesmaids and hens
Outfits and accessories for bridesmaids

For the groom
Choosing best man, ushers and stags
Suits for the groom's party
Transport for the wedding party
First-night accommodation

To choose/book together

Wedding planner, if you're having one

Venues and marquees, including decoration

Photographers and videographers

Entertainment: music, DJ, fireworks, kids' minder/entertainer

Catering: menu, wedding cake, favours, chocolate fountain

Jewellers

Invitations and seating plan

The honeymoon

Remember, there will always be certain things that your fiancée will have to do by herself – buying the wedding dress for one! So don't feel left out, and show an active interest.

But it's not all down to just you and your fiancée. Your parents are bound to want to help and get involved. As the groom, you will have a best man and at least one usher helping you on the day. Remember, these guys are working for you out of friendship.

Only delegate to people you know are practical, organised and reliable. Don't just leave them to it: keep in touch and offer support. Set deadlines for when certain tasks or bookings must be done by. Make sure that once a task is completed, you are informed about it.

And finally, don't lose perspective! Try to keep a sense of humour and remind yourself what it's really all about.

TOP TIPS

Here are some pointers to help you have a stress-free engagement and wedding.

- Planning, planning, planning. Make sure you've got all bases covered.
- Compromise. Give in on some of the small things to get what you want on the big things.
- Understanding. Be very understanding. Your bride has dreamed about this day for years.
- Remember that you are important too, so don't always let yourself get railroaded!
- Money: the biggest cause of pre-wedding arguments. Stick to your budget.
- Rely on friends and family for practical and moral support. You can't do it all yourselves.

CHAPTER 5

THE GUEST LIST

It's never too early in the wedding-planning process to start talking about your guest list. This is frequently the first item on the agenda that can cause arguments. Unless you've got a limitless budget and a gigantic venue, then compromises are probably going to have to be made. And remember, it's not just about who you and your fiancée want to come. Both sets of parents will need to invite people too – although hopefully this will largely be relatives and family friends whom you would want there as well. So, before you announce that you're having 250 people and start verbally inviting everyone you know, read this chapter and discuss all the options between yourselves and with your parents.

Selecting who gets an invite and who doesn't can be one of the trickiest tasks in planning your wedding. By now, you and your fiancée should already have decided on roughly what style and size of wedding you want.

You should also be well under way with your research into possible venues, although venues and guest lists can be a bit of a 'chicken and egg' situation. For example, one of the first questions any venue is going to ask you is how many guests you intend to have, so it's advisable to have a good idea of this figure before making appointments to see venues.

Conversely, the number of guests you can invite is ultimately going to be limited by the capacity of your venues – for both ceremony and reception. It's no good spending weeks compiling your perfect guest list of 200, only to find that all local venues can only take up to 125 people. So, having a general idea of these capacities in advance is a good idea. Most wedding venues will give this information on their website. Remember, the number of guests a venue can accommodate will vary according to what part of the venue you are using, and what type of meal you will be offering.

And finally, your budget may well be a decisive factor. Venues will most likely offer a package deal on a price-per-head basis. You will have set yourself a budget for how much you can spend on the reception, and with the best will in the world, you just may have to reduce your number of guests accordingly.

WHO'S IN AND WHO'S OUT

Rather like when you brainstormed your ideas for your wedding (see pages 31–4), you need to start thinking about your guest list in three separate categories.

1. Who is absolutely essential?
- yourself and your bride!
- both sets of parents
- immediate family

- bridesmaids
- best man and ushers
- any other truly essential relatives or closest friends
- the celebrant, vicar, Registrar?

2. Who do you really want to invite?
- other family members
- other friends and old school friends
- your closest work colleagues

3. Anyone else – if you have room
- distant relatives
- more casual friends and acquaintances
- other work colleagues
- anyone you may not be particularly close to, but feel an obligation to in some way

Of course, there will probably be a few people who don't quite fit in to any of these categories, but do the best you can. You may, or may not want to consider creating a fourth category – those people you definitely do *not* want to invite! This could be a contentious issue, particularly if you put your bride's best friend on this list. Other people that may make it on to this list may include:
- people who drink too much and cannot handle their alcohol
- the children of your guests
- ex-boyfriends and ex-girlfriends

DIVIDING THE INVITES
Ideally, your guest list should roughly comprise a 50:50 balance between guests of the bride and her family, and guests of the groom and his family. Alternatively, perhaps if you and your fiancée share the exact same bunch of friends and will thus be doubling up, you may split the allocation three ways: a third for you – the couple, and a third for each set of parents.

This allocation is important, not only to ensure that neither side feels overwhelmed or left out, but also to ensure a happy mix on the day. The last thing you want is a group of six people sitting in the corner, not knowing or mixing with anyone else.

As I've said, both sets of parents need to have a say too, especially if they are paying for much of the event. Ask them each to compile a list under the same headings. When you combine these three lists – the list from you and your fiancée, your parents, and her parents – you are bound to have come out with far too many people. Now begins the tricky job of whittling it down to a realistic figure – realistic for your venue, and your budget.

TRIMMING YOUR GUEST LIST

Your budget/venue dictates that you can only have 100 people. However, you've still got 130 on the list, and it's only getting bigger! What do you do?

Time to prioritise. List your family and people who are friends to both of you. These are your most important guests. Then split whatever is left between your side and that of your fiancée. For example, if all the important guests that you both want to invite add

---

TOP TIPS

Still having problems whittling down your guest list? No one said it would be easy. The process will require tact and sensitivity, both between you and your parents and between you and any people who may feel hurt that they have not been invited. Here are some selection criteria you could apply:

- If you have a large family, cut the list off at aunts and uncles or first cousins. You can then have an informal family reception for any uninvited guests at a later date.
- If a lot of your guests are single, cancel the 'plus one'. With some venues costing around £60 per head, this can really save some money.
- Don't invite children under 18.
- Don't invite colleagues.

up to 60 guests, then you have 40 places available. So the bride's side gets 20 guests and your side gets 20 guests. Sounds simple doesn't it?!

Must I invite everyone who invited me?

Generally as a rule, if you haven't kept in regular touch with someone whose wedding you attended, do not feel obliged to invite them to yours.

Do we have to invite children?

You are not under any obligation to invite children. It is perfectly OK to make this clear when sending out your invitations. Remember though that you may have friends and family who might find it difficult to arrange childcare for both the full day and the evening do.

Is it OK to invite singles without the 'plus one'?

This is a question that crops up frequently. It is perfectly acceptable to invite single people without their dates. After all, you and your fiancée will be paying anything between £25 and £75 per head for dinner, and I don't know many people who would buy dinner for a stranger. If you do go this route, make extra effort when arranging your seating plan to ensure that these singles are seated with friendly and compatible people.

Should I invite people I know cannot attend?

Consider this rule of thumb: if you would like people to know that they are included within your wedding plans, send them an invitation. The decision whether to attend your wedding should be left to them. You may well be surprised at who might make an appearance. But, if you have, for example, elderly or frail relatives whom you know will not be able attend, nevertheless, make sure you send them an invitation to show they have not been forgotten – they will appreciate the gesture.

Invitations to different parts of the day

As you've realised by now, there are several different components to your wedding day: the ceremony, the meal at the reception, and the evening entertainment at the reception. You don't have to invite *all* your guests to *all* parts of the wedding day. Although it may make it more complicated than it's worth, inviting some guests to only some parts may help you invite more people overall. Again, think very careful when doing this – you don't want to make some guests feel like second-class citizens.

But it can work in some cases. Perhaps that frail elderly relative would be up to attending the church service, but would find the hustle and bustle of the reception too much. Perhaps you could invite work colleagues to the evening festivities only.

CO-WORKERS

If you've decided that you just can't afford to invite all your co-workers due to financial constraints, don't be afraid to tell them. Just let them know that you don't want to hurt their feelings but have decided to invite immediate family only. Don't worry – most people will understand.

If you've decided to include your co-workers and you work in a small place of business (and are relatively close to all of them!), then invite them all. Don't leave someone out; it may cause tension in the workplace.

If you work in a large office and only want to invite a few people, make sure you ask your invited guests to be discreet about it. You don't want to create an awkward situation for your colleagues.

Not sure whether to invite the big boss? If you have a good relationship with him/her, why not? However, you shouldn't feel obliged to invite anyone.

THE INVITATIONS

OK, so you've finally sorted out the guest list. It is at this point that you realise 'Hey! We have actually got to write, address and send all of these invites!' Well, that's not strictly true. If you stick with tradition, the invites should be sent out by the bride's parents. If you wish to involve both sets of parents, then you could let each side of the family send out their own invites.

If you are anxious about getting lots of 'unable to attend' replies – perhaps your wedding is at a busy time of year – you may wish to send out 'Save the Date' cards. These do exactly what they say: as soon as you have set your date and booked the venue you notify your intended guests to keep that date free, informing them that full invitations will be sent out nearer the time.

Your invites should reflect the overall style and tone of your wedding. The range of designs available nowadays is huge, ranging from the classic, traditional ivory card, to funky illustrated modern ones and hand-made invitations. Remember, the first impression of what type of wedding your guests will be attending is given when your invite drops onto their mat, so choosing the right invites is important. On the other hand, how many of your guests do you really think are going to keep the invitations? You may wish to consider how much money you are prepared to spend on something that will ultimately end up in the bin in many cases.

Don't forget to co-ordinate. When ordering your invitations from the supplier you may also want to order matching Order of Service cards, Thank You cards (for acknowledging your wedding gifts), Menu cards and Place Name cards.

What should the invitation include?

The only essential component is the invitation itself. Depending on your budget, you may have two sets of invitations printed up, one for the whole wedding and the other for the evening only. You may also wish to include a reply card to prompt the invitee to reply!

You may need to include other information:
• Written travel directions, by road, train and bus.
• Maps showing the venue locations and nearby parking.
• Information on local hotels and B&Bs.

- A schedule for the day, to help people plan travel, childcare, etc.
- Details of your gift list, or equivalent (see Chapter 6).

THE SEATING PLAN

There will always be that third cousin who wasn't happy and wanted to sit somewhere else. All you can do is think about who will get on and create an interesting mix at each table.
- Always place people male-female-male-female around the tables.
- Try to place single people/those who will not know anyone else on a particularly friendly table.
- Try to mix up the two families a bit. That said, weddings do double up as family reunions, so your seating plan can facilitate this.
- Don't split up couples, especially those with young children to keep an eye on.
- Consider having a separate table for all the older children.
- Place elderly relatives, or those with young children, on tables with easy access in and out, and not near any loudspeakers.

The top table

Who to put on the top table – if you are having one – can be a touchy subject, especially if any parents are estranged or have remarried. Talk to all concerned, long before your wedding day. Partners of the best man and chief bridesmaid sit at other tables.

Front of table, facing guests							
CHIEF BRIDESMAID	FATHER OF GROOM	MOTHER OF BRIDE	GROOM	BRIDE	FATHER OF BRIDE	MOTHER OF GROOM	BEST MAN

How do we get our guests talking?

Try hiring a magician to visit the tables during dinner. You could write humourous facts or questions about the guests on the place-name cards. Disposable cameras can be good ice-breakers.

CHAPTER 6
THE GIFT LIST

As you would expect, friends and family will want to give you a present to mark this special occasion and help you set out on married life with all the gear you need! Creating a wedding-gift list ensures that you are not given the same present twice, and enables your guests to buy a gift with the confidence that it is something you definitely want. On the other hand, some couples today feel that a gift list is too materialistic, and, since 70 per cent of you will already have been living together, you will probably not need a complete dinner service and set of saucepans anyway. But not to worry, there are lots of enlightened, eco-friendly and charitable alternatives to gift lists. This chapter will help you find what's right for you. Whichever way you go, make sure this is something you and your fiancée do together.

According to a recent survey of 15,000 brides-to-be and newly-weds, couples have definite views regarding their gift lists. The following statistics emerged:

- Almost 85 per cent like a gift to be bought from their wedding list.
- 98 per cent have created at least one wedding list.
- More than 90 per cent of grooms are involved in creating the wedding list.

WHAT IS A GIFT LIST?

This may seem like a question with a really obvious answer – it's a list of the gifts you want! But there's a bit more to it than that. You don't just type up a list and send it out to your guests. How will they know who has bought what? Where do they go to get it? How do they get it to you? It's not easy to bring a new ironing board or washing machine to a wedding. This is where the professional gift 'service' comes in.

HOW A GIFT-LIST SERVICE WORKS

Gift-list services are traditionally offered by department stores: John Lewis, Debenhams and so forth. They offer a facility whereby you and your fiancée can choose things you want/need from the store, and compile your own unique gift 'wish-list'.

Your guests can then view this list, either in-store, or on-line and buy something from that list. In most cases, they will have the option to leave a personal message to accompany the gift. The list will be regularly updated by the store, so your guests will be able to see what has already been bought, and what is still available.

When you close down your list – usually after your honeymoon, by which time everyone's had a good chance to use it – the retailer will then deliver all the gifts to your door, hopefully all in one go, and hopefully free of charge.

Most couples tend to begin thinking about the gift list about six months before their wedding. Visit a few of the large department stores to get an idea of their stock. Once you have decided upon your retailer, you should try to register your list at least three months before your wedding. Ideally you want to be able to send out details of your gift list along with your wedding invitations.

How to register a gift list

Once you have chosen your department store, visit their wedding-gift department, usually on one of the upper floors, and they will help you register. You will be asked to select the gifts that you would like to add to your gift list from anywhere within the store. The store then creates the list for you, which you can send to your guests with your invites. Alternatively, you can refer your guests to a website. They will usually need to type in the names of the bride and/or groom in order to access the list this way.

INTERNET GIFT SERVICES

You may already have noticed one major drawback to the gift service described above: it limits you to the products of only one store. This was fine back in the days when you needed a job-lot of absolutely everything, from pillow cases to the proverbial kitchen sink. But nowadays, couples are marrying at an older age, may well already be living together, and thus already have the items that featured on a traditional gift list.

Many internet-based companies, such as the market leader, wrapit.co.uk., now cater for couples with more specific or individual requirements. The principles work exactly the same as conventional department-store gift lists. You select the gifts that you would like to receive, which are then compiled into an on-line gift registry. You simply tell your guests the web site to visit, together with your account name and, Bob's your uncle, they select the gift they would like to purchase, pay it for it online, and the gift-list company delivers it to your chosen address.

The big difference is that they can source your gifts from a whole range of different retailers. Their service is operated entirely on-line – there is no central store where guests can go to see the gifts.

WEDDING GIFT COSTS

Before you go running off around the store adding hundreds of pounds' worth of Waterford Crystal or the latest Jamie Oliver blender to your wedding list, it's a good idea to remember that the items on your gift list need to fall within a price range that is going to be affordable to all your guests. Not only is it poor etiquette to price 90 per cent of your guests out of the market, but it will make you and your bride look greedy.

TOP TIP

A safe way to think about the items on your gift list is to break them down into price brackets as follows:

- 20 per cent of gifts between £10 and £30
- 50 per cent of gifts between £30 and £50
- 20 per cent of gifts between £50 and £100
- 10 per cent of gifts can be over £100

If you stick roughly to these figures, then there should be something there that everyone can afford. You thus stand a better chance of getting everything on your list bought for you.

ALTERNATIVES TO THE TRADITIONAL GIFT LIST

Given that your guests will already probably be forking out on travel, overnight accommodation and new outfits in order to attend your wedding – and that a select few will also have had the expense (and fun, of course!) of a stag/hen do –some couples feel uncomfortable expecting their guests to buy them a gift as well.

But there are many alternatives to consider. Perhaps you specify in your invitation material that you do not expect gifts, but will have a donation 'post-box' at the wedding, where guests can make donations – perhaps towards your honeymoon.

Alternatively, you may decide to do something charitable or ecological to commemorate your wedding: sponsor children in the developing world, train a guide dog puppy, or plant some trees.

CHAPTER 7

THE GROOM'S PARTY

At last! The first of several chapters truly devoted to you, the groom! Marriage is a rite of passage, so you need to have your closest friends around you. Your fiancée will have no trouble finding excuses to go with her girlfriends to the bridal shop, the dressmaker's, the hairdresser's, the spa, and the like. So this is a time for you to be bonding with your mates too. And don't forget to include your dad in some of these pre-wedding activities, even if it's just the odd 'lads' drinks' in the local pub. He may not show it, but it's going to be a big deal for him witnessing his son embarking on married life, and perhaps eventually starting a family of his own. But, most importantly, you've got to choose your best man and ushers. They have lots of responsibilities, so choose wisely. Read on.

THE BEST MAN
Just what *is* a best man?

Traditionally, the best man is a bachelor who, should the groom not turn up, stands in for the groom and marries the bride! Luckily, that part of job hasn't been enforced for over 100 years.

So, who is the best man? For a start, he no longer has to be single. He is someone close to the groom, whom the groom trusts to be his right-hand man. He may be a brother, close friend, cousin or his father. These days, the best man could even be the best woman.

The job entails a lot more than just standing around looking good in a suit and chatting up the bridesmaids. The best man is there as the groom's adviser, he keeps the groom organised; helps with planning the wedding; helps seat guests at the wedding; will be in charge of the ushers; will probably need to act as a 'master of ceremonies', announcing the different stages of the day; and generally keeping everyone moving. He should expect to be an all-round trouble-shooter on the day. So there is a lot more to it than first meets the eye. If you have already been a best man yourself, then you should know what it is you are looking for.

Choosing your best man

Most of us probably think that picking a best man is easy. In some cases, it really is as easy as asking your only brother or your best friend of 20 years; there is no other choice, and everyone knows it.

But, if there is more than one candidate, how do you choose the right man for the job? This is where it can get tricky. It's not just a question of gut instinct or emotional ties. You need to think carefully about who will do the best job on the day – and this may not necessarily be the person you feel closest to.

True story

I attended a wedding a few years ago where the groom had, naturally enough, asked his only brother to be his best man. The trouble was, this best man lived in Canada, while everybody else was based in the UK. Through no fault of his own, he'd had no opportunity to meet the ushers, or his brother's friends. On top of this, unfortunately, he had few social graces. He mumbled his speech, and showed little initiative when it came to keeping the ball rolling. Thankfully, one of the ushers – the bride's brother – saw what was happening, and very subtly stepped into the breach. The day was saved, without any offence being caused.

The above should serve as a cautionary tale! Short of asking for CVs and holding interviews, you need to look at the pros and cons of all your 'candidates'. It will be easier to appease one friend initially offended that you haven't chosen him, than 100 guests appalled at a best man who *seriously* misbehaves on the day.

You will not be doing your closest friend any favours by choosing him for a role he is patently unequal to. Out of loyalty he would, no doubt, do his best; but this may still end up being excruciating for you all. Instead, find a way for him to still play an active role – as an usher, perhaps – with less *public* responsibility.

Is he sober...ish?!

This one seems like a 'no-brainer', but it is quite amazing how many wedding days are tainted by the best man slurring his way through his speech, spilling wine all over the bride, or making inappropriate passes at the bride's spinster aunt. I was at a Scottish wedding last year where the best man thought, in his drunken state, that it was a good idea to stand on the top table to give his speech. It was only when all the guests pointedly looked down at the floor that we realised he was a 'true Scot' (not wearing underwear under his kilt). So, if your best man likes a drink, then he *must* be able to wait, or at the very least hold off until after the duties and speeches are concluded, before getting truly plastered, being blown out by all the bridesmaids and dancing like a prat.

Is he reliable?

There are so many things for your best man to remember and keep track of, both on the day, and in the planning stages, that reliability is paramount. From organising the stag do to remembering the wedding rings, you are placing a lot of trust and responsibility in this person. Finding out on your wedding day that he has lost the rings is not an option. I know this sounds like a cliché, but, believe me, it does happen.

Is he punctual and organised?

With nerves kicking in, you may well forget to put on underwear, let alone turn up to the church on time. This is when the best man should jump into action. It is his job to make sure that you are dressed, ready, and on time. If you suddenly express a wish to drive to Harrogate and say hello to your old English teacher, it is up to him to persuade you that, actually, going to bed is the better option.

On the day, it will be, partially at least (hopefully your venue co-ordinator will be active here too), up to him to keep things on schedule. Needless to say, he therefore needs a schedule to follow...

Is he presentable?

After you and your bride, the best man is probably the most conspicuous person at your wedding. He is a reflection on you, your bride, your families – your whole wedding. While you and his other close friends may forgive, or be accustomed to his foibles, the majority of your guests will never have met him before.

The last thing you want is to have a best man with personal hygiene problems or a dubious sense of personal style and grooming. Don't forget that his image is going to be preserved for all eternity in the wedding photos you have spent thousands of pounds on. If his everyday style leaves a lot to be desired, then maybe it is not a good idea to even entertain the idea of having him as your best man.

Is he diplomatic and sociable?

Please see the cautionary tale on pages 59–60! Your best man needs to have good communication skills, since conversing with your guests, whether they are known to him or not, will be essential. He will need to be able to mix with a variety of people, to think on his feet. Initiative and presence are perhaps the key words here.

Can he speak in public?

Whilst there are also speeches from the bride's father and, of course, you, the groom, the best man's speech is general regarded as the highlight speech. This said, he doesn't need to be a professional after-dinner speaker, or have a 'Home-Counties' posh accent; but having some personality, a sense of humour, and being able to string a sentence together is pretty essential. Depending on how much you trust him, you may want him to run his speech ideas by you first!

THE BEST MAN'S DUTIES

Ultimately, the best man's duties are whatever the groom says they are. However, unless you are prepared to jeopardise this friendship for life then you will remember that this friend is performing this duty as an unpaid favour. So don't push your luck! But, if you have chosen wisely, you have chosen a best man who will go the distance for you. Playing safe, tradition would suggest that his duties include:

• Helping you with your pre-wedding planning.

• Organising the stag night, ensuring you come to no (permanent!) harm. See Chapter 8 for further details.

• Accompanying you throughout your wedding day (see Chapter 9), helping you to relax, getting you to the ceremony on time...

• Managing your ushers, ensuring they fulfil their duties. You will be too busy to do this on the day, believe me!

• Collecting and distributing the buttonholes for the groom's party.

• Collecting the Orders of Service; presenting them to your guests, whether in person, or by ensuring that they are placed in the seats.

• Carrying the wedding rings.

• Generally, throughout the day: discreetly hovering, making sure your needs are catered for. This said, he should have the tact to recognise when to give you and your bride some privacy!

• Ensuring that guests have lifts to the reception after the ceremony.
• Making his speech; reading out messages and telegrams from those unable to attend.
• Ensuring that transport for the bride and groom after the reception is on hand. The best man should look after your travel documents until you need them.
• Returning all hired suits back to the hire shop.
• Organising the safe transportation of any wedding gifts from the venue to the home of the couple or their parents.

THE USHERS

The groom, with the help of his best man, chooses the ushers who can be anyone attending the wedding but who usually are brothers or friends of the groom. As a rule, you should have an usher for every 35 to 40 guests. The best man must ensure that the ushers know what their duties are on the day.

THE USHERS' DUTIES

• Arrive at the ceremony venue early, before the groom.
• Collect the Orders of Service; make sure the officiant has a copy. Leave service sheets at the end of the front rows for the bridesmaids. Distribute the Orders of Service to guests as they arrive.
• Distribute buttonholes to all the guests as they arrive.
• Should it be raining, be at hand with umbrellas to escort guests into the ceremony venue.
• All ushers should wait for the guests on the left side of church entrance. Once they have greeted the guests, they need to advise them on any restrictions concerning confetti or photography.
• The head usher stands by the church door and gives out the service sheets. A second usher stands at the top of the aisle and, if he does not recognise a guest, politely asks whether he or she is a guest of the bride or the groom. The bride's family and guests are seated to the left of the aisle and the groom's to the right.

• A third usher is positioned halfway down the aisle to show guests to their seats. The first two rows of seating are reserved for close family members. When the groom and best man arrive, they wait in the front row, with the groom's parents occupying the second row on the right. The mother of the bride occupies the front row on the left, with a space beside her for the bride's father. The usher should escort any lone guests to their seats, politely offering his arm to single ladies.

• A fourth usher (you will need a fourth usher if your wedding party exceeds 120 people) waits at the entrance: he has the responsibility of escorting the bride's mother to her seat.

• When everyone is seated, the ushers take their places near the back of the church and quietly escort any latecomers to the nearest seats.

• After the service, ushers are responsible for supervising the guests' transport to the reception. The last usher to leave should make a quick check of the church to make sure no property has been left behind.

• It is very important that the best man fully explain to each usher exactly what his duties are; it's probably a good idea to give them a typed up list of duties and a schedule for the day.

WHAT ARE YOU ALL GOING TO WEAR?

Wedding magazines seem to focus on the bride's dress, and far less on the groom's, best man's and ushers' suits. The right suit makes almost as much impact on the day as the bride's dress, so make sure that you take the time to find the right colour, style and, most importantly, the right fitting suit. An uncomfortable fidgety man doesn't make for a happy day, or for good wedding pictures. The suit should be properly accessorised. Talk to your bride, to ensure the suits are in keeping with the style of the bride's dress.

Most wedding suits are hired to keep costs down, but also because you are not likely to wear it again. With all the new styles and designs, it is not that difficult for all the guys to look both classy and individual on the wedding day.

What are your options?

- **Morning dress**. This is the traditional morning coat with top hat and waistcoat. Ideal for grand and church weddings, but can look too much at smaller or more modern ceremonies.
- **Lounge suit**. The classic flattering shape. Black always looks smart, but grey and dark blue work too. Choose a solid-coloured silk tie, perhaps one that coordinates with the bride's dress.
- **Fashion suit**. This is an option if more formal suits just don't suit your modern or urban venues. But proceed with caution. Any fashion faux pas will be captured for all eternity in your photos.
- **Dinner jacket/black tie**. This is the style usually worn in America. Technically it's evening dress, so probably not a good idea if you're getting married before 5pm. A hired dinner jacket can stick out a mile, so invest in your own. You will be able to wear it again.
- **Highland dress**. For anyone born north of the border. Choose the tartan for your clan. Can be very flamboyant and stylish, and comes with it's own range of accessories.

Make sure it fits

Try the whole suit on a week before the wedding. If you've put on a few pounds, there's still time to get a different size.

- Your suit jacket should fit well and give you a full range of motion, both buttoned and unbuttoned. Remember that you will be dancing, sitting and hugging.
- You should be able to fit one finger between the collar of your shirt and your neck, but no more than that. The shirt cuffs should not ride up when you stretch your arms.
- Your waistcoat should button comfortably and sit just below the waistband of your trousers.
- Trousers should break over the instep, about a third of the way down the shoe. Trousers that are too short can spoil the whole look.
- Lace-up shoes are a must. But break them in before the day, and make sure they are nicely polished.
- Yes, it's a formal occasion, but you need to be comfortable too.

CHAPTER 8

THE STAG DO

Its been called a rite of passage, the last night of freedom and a big old piss-up, but the most important thing to come from any stag do is that it should be an event to remember and be talked about for years to come. Yet if you follow tradition, you will have very little to do with actually organising, or even deciding where you will be going and what you will be doing on your stag do. Luckily, with all the planning and costs involved in today's stag dos, most best men are more than happy for the groom to be involved.

Gone are the days of having a few drinks at your local followed by a meal and a hangover. No, it seems these days that nothing short of a weekend's drinking, partying and debauchery will do. From a few nights in Newquay to a week in Ibiza, nothing is done by half. The toughest part is deciding what to do and where to go. It would be far too simple to invite all your friends to a weekend in New York, but can they afford it? How many people will be going?

Your stag do can be a bit of a double-edged sword. As much as you are looking forward to it, there is always a bit of trepidation as to what your best man has in store for you. This is where you discover if you have chosen the right best man for the job.

WHEN TO HAVE YOUR STAG DO

The best time to go on your stag do is at least a couple of weeks before the big day and, where possible, on the same weekend as your bride's hen party. This means that you and your fiancée won't be losing two weekends of organising time so close to the big day.

TOP TIP

Whatever you do, DO NOT have your stag do the day before the wedding. Turning up late, looking rough, or being ill will be unforgivable.

PLANNING YOUR STAG DO

Traditionally, the groom is kept in the dark about his stag do, which is not great if you don't trust your best man or, worse still, if you gave him a hard time on his stag do. You are guaranteed to receive a few surprises on your stag do, so be prepared.

The only way to ensure that you get the stag do you want is to get together with your best man away from prying ears (i.e., bride and bridesmaids) and discuss all aspects of your stag do: likes, dislikes, boundaries, any activities that you particularly want to do, any places you really want to go to.

Who's invited?

The best man should ask you who you want to attend the stag do. Do you want to invite all and sundry, or just close friends? Will you all enjoy the chosen activity? Will the stags all get on with each other? If you're not sure, then have a back-up or standby list. What about your father and the bride's brother?

It is often the most unlikely person who raises eyebrows on a stag do. A perfect example is my own stag do in Las Vegas. We had the usual suspects of friends and colleagues, but it was my fiancée's Uncle Cliff who really surprised everyone.

Cliff works for the local council, plays bridge every Thursday and hadn't even been abroad for 10 years. But within two hours of hitting the tables, Cliff was partying LARGE, drinking, gambling and ending up at 4 a.m. in a lap-dancing club throwing $20 bills around like they were monopoly money. But hey, What Happens in Vegas Stays in Vegas, so I can't tell you any more than that. But it just goes to show, the most unlikely stag can make a difference.

Can everyone afford it?

Stag weekends can cost up to £600 per person nowadays, especially if you are planning a foreign trip, so it is imperative that you make sure all stags attending can afford it. The best man may end up being owed a small fortune if the lads don't have enough money with them on the day, and this can cause ill feeling amongst you all.

Depending on where you are going, the correct etiquette is that the groom doesn't pay for the stag do. However, this is usually unrealistic if you are travelling abroad. The best man should ensure that people pay up front for the bulk of the costs, and all bring a minimum amount of cash with them. It may be a good idea to have a whip round for a general kitty/beer fund.

Does everyone like the same activities?

If you are planning on going out on the lash for two days with no sleep, there seems little point of inviting a teetotaller. Likewise, if you are planning an activity weekend, it's probably not a good idea to invite the bride's 65-year old father who has a gammy leg. Okay, these are extreme examples, but you do want everyone to be able to join in and enjoy themselves.

DECIDING WHAT TO DO

You will need to take into account budget, distance, travel restrictions, visas, how long you intend to stay and availability.

With most stag dos now covering at least a weekend, the choice of where to go and how to get there is massive, with hundreds of stag- and hen-planning companies offering a choice of packages and destinations in the UK as well as abroad.

Drinking and partying

Is the cliché of a stag do your idea of the perfect weekend? Drinking from dusk to dawn, lap-dancing clubs, curry houses – oh, and suffering the inevitable hangovers. If it is, make sure that you invite only the type of people that enjoy that sort of weekend.

Culture and local cuisine

Maybe one of the culture capitals of Europe is the perfect destination, with amazing architecture and restaurants. Many of Europe's cities are great value for money and easy to get to.

Sports weekend

If you enjoy a game of golf, then the warmer climates of southern Europe are perfect. Golfing in Spain is one of the top stag-weekend activities, but be aware some of the top courses in Marbella charge over £100 per round. What about a day at the races, or clay-pigeon shooting?

Adrenaline-junky weekend

For some of you, a weekend of drinking just doesn't hit the spot. You need a challenge, something that tests you and gives you an adrenaline rush. This is the fastest growth area in the stag market. Rock-climbing courses are great fun, and white-water rafting is always a blast. What about sky-diving, paint-balling, racing-car driving – the list is endless.

TOP 10 STAG DESTINATIONS IN THE UK

The UK still has a fantastic tradition of stag nights and, let's face it, not everyone wants to, or can afford to go abroad. Pubs, clubs, lap-dancing and ending up in a curry house are all rites of passage for UK stags. Here are the top 10 places to visit on your stag night, based on how many clubs, pubs and places to eat are in the area.

1. Nottingham. No. 1 for a good reason. Everything in this town is large, with 50 bars and 20 clubs for starters! There is a notable lack of snobbery and pretentiousness in Nottingham and everyone is welcome, falling from one great bar to another, followed by some breathtaking clubs to finish the evening.

2. Newquay. Surf, sea and drinking, with pubs and restaurants offering outside drinking and dining for most of the year. The bars and clubs reflect the varied styles and tastes of the constantly changing clientele. There is a promenade – always a cliché for a stag do – and a pedestrianised zone filled with a lively nightlife.

3. Manchester. Famous for being the club capital of the UK in the early 1990s, the Manchester of today is somewhat different from its past portrayal in the newspapers. There are some fantastic hotels, bars and clubs, and a couple of world-renowned lap-dancing clubs.

4. Leeds. Leeds city centre alone has upwards of 90 restaurants and cafés, 21 major hotels, four theatres and over 180 pubs and bars.

5. London. Our great capital city has something for everyone. Covent Garden is always a good place to start, with its cafés, bars and eateries. You are spoilt for choice for late-night entertainment.

6. Brighton. For such a tolerant, open culture, it is surprising that a lot of places refuse stag dos. If you are going with a small group then this could be a good bet.

7. Edinburgh. No one drinks like the Scots (well, maybe the Irish), but you just cannot go wrong with this vibrant cosmopolitan city. It has friendly, welcoming places to eat, drink and be merry. And it can be the gateway to some highland pursuits, enabling you to combine outdoor activities with the more traditional pub crawl.

8. Newcastle. Everyone just loses the plot here on a Friday and Saturday night, and it is easy to understand why, with rows and rows of pubs on almost every street in the city centre.

9. Birmingham. Up and coming for stags, Birmingham has some of the best curry houses and a really modern city centre.

10. Cardiff. A new kid on the block but well worth looking at after the regeneration of the city centre. This city has some really cutting edge restaurants and bars.

GOING ABROAD

It seems that every time I go to Stansted airport there is always a group of lads dressed in stag-weekend T-shirts or hats, excitedly waiting to get the festivities started. The low-cost airline boom is the prime reason that over 48 per cent of stags now go abroad on their stag weekends. And with the cheap hotels, food and beer in a lot of the former eastern-bloc countries, it is sometimes cheaper to go abroad than to one of the UK cities.

Choosing your destination

How do you choose where to go for an overseas stag do? Choice of destination is obviously the most important decision – I mean, this is supposed to be the party weekend to end all weekends.

The eastern-bloc countries are a destination of choice due mainly to how cheap they are to visit. A pint of beer can cost as little as 50 pence and hotel rooms start from £20 per night. The old favourites (Amsterdam, Barcelona and Dublin) are best set up to receive large groups of (drunk, in most cases) men. Perhaps it is your chosen activity – skiing or rock-climbing, for example – that determines the destination for you.

Price is the biggest single deciding factor on destination for most stags, so why not set a budget that you think everyone can afford and work from there. The average cost per person for a standard one-night, two-day weekend to Europe is £175 based on low-cost airline flights, a two- or three-star hotel with two people sharing and transport to and from the airport. (These figures are subject to change and will go up or down depending on hotel prices, etc.). Don't forget you've got the costs of food, drink and entertainment when you get there.

TOP 10 STAG DESTINATIONS ABROAD

1. Prague, Czech Republic. Prague has all the right ingredients for a great stag do. Everyone is welcome at most of the hundreds of bars and clubs in Prague. But remember to go easy on the absinthe!

2. Riga, Latvia. As the largest city in the Baltic states, with a population of 800,000, Riga is the perfect choice for those looking for cheap hotels, beer and entertainment. It is less than three hours flight from the UK and is serviced by the low-cost airlines. It has a vibrant nightlife and is by far the most popular city in the whole of the Baltics.

3. Budapest, Hungary. With its Turkish baths, eclectic architecture and grand old coffeehouses, Budapest has enough attractions to entertain visitors all year round. After the summer influx of tourists, locals reclaim their capital in the autumn, when the cultural season starts up again. Add a lively nightlife, rapidly improving gastronomy and excellent high-end hotels, and you will be in for a fabulous time.

4. Amsterdam, Holland. Amsterdam is party, party, party all night. We all know about the smoking bars and the strip clubs. The bars are usually open until 4 a.m. on Fridays and Saturdays and until 2 a.m. on other days. This is a mad place to visit if you have never done so.

5. Barcelona, Spain. Spain takes three places out of the top 10, with Barcelona the highest, with shows, bars, discotheques, concerts, terraces and popular fiestas just a few of the choices that the city offers for enjoying the Mediterranean night.

6. Dublin, Ireland. In the past few years Dublin has tried to ban stag parties altogether, but not-to-be-deterred stags from around the globe have continued to swarm there in their thousands. Great for everything and 10/10 for atmosphere.

7. Marbella, Spain. Made famous by the excesses of the 1990's and being the place to see and be seen, Marbella really is all about one small marina. Puerto Banus is the only place to party with its multimillion-pound yachts, world famous bars and night clubs galore, but, and there is always a but, it is a pricey place to play in, so be careful if you are on a budget.

8. Frankfurt, Germany. Stunning skylines, historic buildings and art galleries . . . Oh right, sorry, it also has more different types of strong beer than any city in the world, a great party attitude and loads of amazing hotels.

9. Ibiza, Balearics. Hot weather, fantastic beaches and the coolest clubs on the planet. Ibiza is made for a party weekend; it is a good idea to book tickets to the more famous clubs before you leave the UK, as that will save time hunting around when you get there.

10. Moscow, Russia. With cheap flights, good restaurants and great bars, Moscow is now the hip place to go on your stag weekend. Moscow has something for everyone and, of course, as much vodka as you can imagine. But stay safe, and respect local customs. Moscow is my No. 1 recommendation for stag parties looking for something new.

ORGANISING AN OVERSEAS STAG DO

There are quite a lot of factors to take into consideration when planning a stag do abroad – things that you wouldn't need to worry about for a local night or weekend in the UK. So this is where having a capable best man is important.

• Plan ahead. You don't have long in your destination, so find out which bars, clubs and restaurants are the best for your party. Do your homework by using guidebooks such as the Lonely Planet or Rough Guide series. Use the Internet to research potential destinations.

• Check to see if you need jabs.

• Put one responsible person – presumably the best man – in charge of looking after the tickets. This saves one of you losing your ticket and everyone else getting pissed off.

• Carry written confirmation of all bookings and reservations.

• Make sure everyone knows the name and address of the hotel you are staying at.

• Try to learn a few words and phrases of the local language.

• Make sure everyone has both UK and foreign currency on them. It can be a good idea to have a contingency fund from the start – again, looked after by someone responsible. That way, should you all run out of money, at least you have enough to get to the airport and have a bite to eat.

• Security levels have remained high since the 9/11 attacks, and security measures at airports have been increased which take extra time. So do make sure you allow plenty of time for getting to the airport and checking in.

• It will be tempting to have a pint or two at the airport in order to get the ball rolling, but airlines and their staff are increasingly strict about letting inebriated passengers travel, so drink in moderation. Spare a thought for your fellow passengers. If you seriously

TOP TIP

The best advice when travelling abroad is 'DON'T LEAVE YOUR COMMON SENSE AT HOME.' Everyone wants to have a good time and enjoy the local hospitality, but remember, in different countries there are different acceptable levels of behaviour. Try to find out about any strange laws that are in force at your chosen destination. For instance, in Faliraki, Greece, the laws on nudity in public are being enforced strongly, so getting tied naked to a lamp post is a no-no, as you could end up in jail.

misbehave during the flight, you could even be faced with a lawsuit! I'm sure this isn't the sort of lasting memory of your stag do that you have in mind.

• Get adequate travel insurance for your trip. Health care abroad is notoriously expensive. Don't forget any sporting or high-risk activities will probably require extra insurance. It will be cheaper to buy the insurance as one job lot for the whole group, rather than on an individual basis.

PROHIBITED ITEMS FOR TRAVEL

Check with your airline for a definitive list of what you can and cannot carry on your person, in your hand luggage and in your checked baggage. These lists can change all the time, but they generally include:

• toy guns (plastic or metal) and catapults.
• metal knives of any length, including pen knives, letter openers, or knives made of any other material (such as polycarbonate or ceramic) that is strong enough to be used as a potential weapon.
• metal cutlery and corkscrews.
• razor blades (unless fixed like a disposable razor).
• tradesmen's tools, such as screwdrivers, that have the potential to be used as weapons.
• scissors, including manicure scissors (except where both blades are round-ended).
• hypodermic syringes (unless required for medical reasons, such as diabetes). You may need to carry some documentation – a copy of a prescription, for example, to prove that you have a genuine need.
• knitting needles or darts.
• large sporting bats and clubs (such as baseball, softball and cricket bats, and golf clubs; tennis, badminton and squash rackets are okay). If you are undertaking a sporting activity when you're abroad, ideally you want to arrange a deal where any necessary equipment is provided at the location as part of the activity package.
• billiard, snooker or pool cues.

RESPECT AND REPUTATIONS

Have a drink. Hell, have ten, it's your stag do after all! But the problem is, stag-goers have earned themselves a bit of a bad reputation when it comes to behaviour abroad and, more often than not, they end up drowning themselves in drink, swearing at strangers and puking on pavements. Mm, lovely!

It's hard not to turn every night into a bit of a session, but many overseas authorities are now catching on to the kind of problems young tourists can bring to their countries and, like it or not, they're starting to crack down. This means having to do a bit of swotting up before you go. In most countries it just means using your common sense. Before you end up in a crumpled, drunken mess on the side of the pavement (or in a police cell), it is always a good idea to learn a little about the local customs and laws so you can blend in rather than stand out while you're there.

This may all sound a bit draconian, but when you think about how many of us descend on popular stag destinations each year, all set to party until we drop, it doesn't take long for a stunning paradise to turn into a slovenly backwater. Have fun, but show respect, too.

Stop to think about the local people in the area where you are staying and how your presence there affects them. Although you know that the abuse you are shouting at your mate is tongue in cheek, locals may not.

Think about the impact so many people arriving in your town would have, and act accordingly – don't play up and make yourselves extra conspicuous, just for the sake of it. Don't think that because you're not in your home town or country you can get away with bad behaviour. You may not. Remember that the laws in the country you are visiting will often be entirely different to the ones you are used to at home. Acting like you are still at home could get you into all kinds of trouble.

Don't just assume that people will clear up your mess. Be responsible for your own litter. Yes, that includes empty vodka bottles and the wrapper from that final take-away – put them in the rubbish bin.

Rolling around half naked on the beach may be your idea of fun, but the local policeman may disagree. Check out the local customs and dress codes even if no laws are in place. Not respecting customs can cause offence.

DO NOT TAKE DRUGS. Getting arrested and imprisoned is not anyone's idea of a good stag do, whether in the UK or abroad.

ON THE DAY

Say a prayer, and enjoy yourself! The most difficult thing is not fading, so pace yourself. Assuming that there will be lots of alcohol involved, don't get blind drunk early on in the proceedings.

Depending on your destination and activity, there may be other things you can do in order to ensure that everyone enjoys themselves. It may sound a bit lacking in spontaneity, but giving a written itinerary to each stag could be a good idea. Be assured, when you, or another stag wake up under a tree with no-one else in sight, you'll be grateful for that piece of paper that's got the best man's mobile number on it, the number of a local taxi firm, and the address of the hotel you're staying at.

Since you're the common factor among all the members of your stag party, make sure you enjoy their company and help everyone to get along. You will have invited all your ushers, so if they haven't all met each other before this is the ideal opportunity for them to get to know each other and build a rapport. They are all going to have to get on and work together on the wedding day.

If you are participating in any sporting or high-risk activity, you will want to keep the drinking till later. Follow the instructions and safety procedures of your guide/activity leader. Don't be tempted to show off. Your bride will not want to help you hobble down the aisle with your leg in plaster.

And finally, the evidence. Make sure any cameras are in the hands of people you trust!

CHAPTER 9

THE WEDDING DAY

The big day is finally here. This is where you find out if all the hard work, sweat and tears have paid off. The last thing you want today of all days is for any last-minute problems or oversights to surface. That said, weddings seem to have a knack for attracting the unexpected, and you may have to take the odd little hitch in your stride. Your wedding day is an exciting and anxious time so you can be forgiven for being a bit forgetful and preoccupied. To avoid losing the plot over something small, the checklist in this chapter will help you cover all the bases.

TRY TO REMAIN CALM

Easier said than done, I know. I mean, this is your wedding day after all, and it is perfectly natural to be nervous or anxious! The main thing to remember is that all grooms feel like this on the day of their wedding, and if anyone tells you different then they are lying or trying to make you feel better. Talk to your best man about any specific worries that you have – he is your right-hand man, and it is his job to do any last-minute trouble-shooting or alleviate any anxieties.

The one thing not to do at any time before the ceremony is to have a drink or five to calm your nerves. Turning up at the altar two sheets to the wind or smelling like a beer cellar is a sure-fire way to ruin your wedding day. That said, I have been to plenty of weddings where the groom has had a quiet, civilised drink with his best man and ushers beforehand, perhaps in the pub round the corner from the church, and it wasn't a problem. The key here is to know yourself, and be disciplined – do make it just the one. Your best man should also be looking out for you here.

CHECKLIST OF ESSENTIALS

This checklist may not solve all of the last-minute glitches, but it will certainly make sure that you do not turn up to your wedding wearing odd socks. Don't leave the house until all items are ticked:

- suit and waistcoat
- shirt – and a spare shirt
- tie, cravat or bow-tie
- cufflinks and watch
- belt, cummerbund or braces, depending on your outfit
- shoes – polished – and check those shoe-laces aren't frayed
- socks and underwear
- handkerchief
- umbrella
- cash, including envelopes (tips for clergy and Registrar, etc.)
- prompt cards for your speech

- legal paperwork
- the wedding rings – give them to the best man
- a fully charged mobile phone, for any last-minute coordination. But remember to turn it off before the ceremony!
- cigarettes and lighter, if you're a smoker
- and thus you should also have mints or breath-freshener
- toiletries and grooming accessories
- contact lenses and eye drops if you wear them
- overnight bag and/or luggage for honeymoon. Ask your best man to make sure it's in your wedding-night hotel room.

GROOMING

Today is the one day you really do want to look your absolute best. But avoid any drastic changes in haircut for the day itself. Go for a trim, a few days to a week beforehand, possibly slightly shorter than usual. If you use hair gel, use slightly less than usual.

If your skin is prone to break outs, be prepared with a treatment. Use moisturiser and a new razor. Go slowly! If you are always cutting yourself when having a wet shave, now might be a good time to try using an electric shaver. And go sparingly with the after shave.

Make sure your teeth are really clean and your breath fresh. Have clean hands and clean and trimmed fingernails. Allow plenty of time to get dressed, and pay attention to the details.

PRE-CEREMONY TIMELINE

Making sure that you are in the right place at the right time can be a tricky thing to do. The best man should be on top of this but just in case here is a timeline for the build-up to the ceremony. Remember the only person that is allowed to be late for the ceremony is, of course, the bride.

As most weddings take place early afternoon, this timeline is based on a 2pm wedding. This is only a guide and must be adjusted according to the time, as well as the type, of your ceremony.

8am You probably don't need an alarm call, but make sure your clock is set anyway. Sleeping late is not an option today.

8.15am Wake up again and thank God for the snooze function. If you haven't had a call from your best man, then give him a call and tell him he has failed the very first task of the day.

9am Have a bath or shower and spend some time on grooming.

9.30am Do your hair, trim your nails, apply any moisturiser or aftershave (do this now and avoid it marking you or your crisp white shirt). Your best man should have arrived by now.

10am Have breakfast with the best man (for this reason, you should not have gotten dressed yet). Go over any last-minute checks and make sure that you eat plenty to keep you going for the day ahead.

10.45am Get dressed. There is nothing like a smart suit to make you feel good, get the butterflies going and build your excitement.

Two to three hours to go. You, your best man and all the ushers meet at the wedding venue. Double check that everything is in place, that everyone knows their duties and, most importantly, that the best man has the rings.

One hour to go. Have a final get-together with your team and thank them for all their hard work. Now is the time to get the ushers and the best man ready to receive your guests.

TOP TIP

I know, I know, it's getting repetitive now. But before you leave for the ceremony, do one last double check of the following:

- Does the best man have the rings?
- Have you got the legal paperwork you need?
- Have you sent your gift to the bride? And a romantic note or text message?
- Do you have the prompt cards for your speech?
- Have you organised the flowers for the mums?
- Have you confirmed the wedding-night accommodation?
- Have you got all tickets and passports for your honeymoon?

Ten minutes to go. One final check that the best man definitely has the rings, then take your position at the front of the venue. Congratulations! In approximately half an hour you will be a happily married man.

THE CEREMONY
In the last few days you should have had a rehearsal of the ceremony, so you should have a good idea of what's coming up. But with all your family and guests around you, and everyone dressed up, plus the wedding-day nerves, it may be a bit overwhelming. Your bride is probably feeling even more nervous, so try and stay calm and reassuring for her sake. And tell her how beautiful she is! Ideally you should have memorised your vows, but don't worry, the celebrant is there to prompt you. You will no doubt want some photographs taken at the church/ceremony venue. Smile and enjoy!

BETWEEN VENUES
If your ceremony and reception are being held in two separate venues, the journey between them will probably be your first private moments as man and wife. Private – except for the chauffeur, horse-and-carriage driver, or helicopter pilot, that is! Since you've arranged the transport, no doubt you will have thought of finishing touches such as champagne and flutes on ice.

AT THE RECEPTION
The receiving line
This is a tradition that many people don't bother with nowadays. The wedding party stand in a line and the guests file past as they arrive. This enables you to be sure that you have spoken to all your guests, and enables them to meet and thank your parents. But it can take a good half hour for 100 people to file past, so make sure drinks are offered to people while they are waiting. If you don't have a receiving line, make sure you and your bride circulate with everyone – when everyone is seated is an ideal time.

The photographs

You will probably have formal group photos taken early on in the reception. Your best man and ushers should help to round people up – politely of course! Your photographer should advise you on the various groups: the happy couple; the groom's party; the bride and her bridesmaids; the families, and so forth. It's a good idea for your groom to have a list of the different groups; he can then announce them as people are needed. Make sure that your other guests are entertained and offered refreshments in the meantime.

The speeches

You probably relaxed after the ceremony, but you're not out of the woods yet. You've still got your speech to deliver! But don't worry, the whole next chapter is designed to help you with this. In any case, the biggest pressure is on the best man and his speech. Make sure you drink in moderation until the speeches are over.

The first dance

Many grooms find this more nerve-wracking than their speech. Traditionally, the first dance is the first public display of partnership between a man and wife. For some, it is a simple slow dance; for others, it's a chance to display their dancing prowess. Choose a song that has meaning for you both. Why not consider booking a course of dance lessons with your bride? Not only will it impress your guests, but it is something you may enjoy doing together to get away from the rigours of planning your wedding.

CHAPTER 10

THE SPEECH

Just when you thought all the hard work was over and you could sit back relax and enjoy the day, it's time for the speeches. The good news is that the weight of expectation is not on the groom – rather, it's on the best man, with everyone waiting to see how badly you (the groom) are going to get stitched up in his speech. Nevertheless, your speech is extremely important to many people – not least your bride. This is probably going to be one of the few times in your marriage when you stand up in public and tell the world what she means to you. So push the boat out. And there are a lot of other people who have helped make this day happen, not least your parents, your best man and the other attendants, and all your guests.

This is your opportunity to express your gratitude. Follow the guidelines in this chapter, and you will be able to give a confident, thoughtful speech.

I have had a hand in planning hundreds of weddings and at some point during the build-up I typically get a call from the groom in varying degrees of stress worried about the speech. A recent study showed that over 65 per cent of people in the UK suffer from glossophobia (a fear of public speaking), so over half the people at your wedding breakfast will understand what you're going through.

I will tell you the same thing that I tell each groom: the key to making a great speech is in the planning. Yes, I know, that's been my mantra throughout this book, but it really is as simple as that. Failing to prepare is to prepare to fail as the saying goes.

In my experience, the only times a speech is received badly or a speaker is embarrassed are when the cardinal rule of speech-making is broken: never, never, never think that you can make it up as you go along. You're going to be standing up in front of your friends, family and up to 100 guests; you are going to be nervous, probably hot, and in an unfamiliar venue; now is not the time to be lost for words. However nervous you are feeling, you need to project confidence. This is made all the easier when you have planned your speech and know what you're going to say and when.

There are three stages to writing a great speech: writing it, rehearsing it and delivering it. So practise enough until you feel comfortable with it and can remember it pretty well. And are you going to play it straight or play it for laughs? If you are not a funny person or never seem to be able to get jokes to sound right, then now is not the time experiment with a stand-up comedy routine.

If you are planning to sprinkle humour into your speech, then you need to practise it together with a close friend or family member to get their feedback. Of course, you will have the good will of your audience on the day, but you still need the core of a funny speech.

The straight speech is always a safe bet. Sometimes a straight speech with an amusing true-life anecdote or witty observation or quotation can be just as good – and entertaining – as a speech that contains full-blown 'jokes'.

ORDER OF SPEECHES

You can have variations on this order if circumstances call for it. Perhaps the bride wants to say a few words too. Perhaps the bride's mother will speak in place of an absent or deceased father. The order in which the speeches traditionally take place is:

• The bride's father, who finishes his speech with a toast to the health of the bride and groom.

• The groom, who responds to the bride's father on behalf of the bride and himself and ends by toasting the bridesmaids and, usually, introducing the best man. During your speech you will also present flowers to the two mothers, and thank-you gifts to the best man, ushers and bridesmaids.

• The best man, who replies on behalf of the bridesmaids and ushers, thanking the bride and groom for their gifts, gives a hilarious speech and reads any telegrams or messages.

THE SEVEN-MINUTE RULE

We have all seen award ceremonies on TV where the recipient of the award gushes on and on and on until finally the music begins to play and the award recipient is dragged offstage. No matter how good the speech, if it goes on too long, attention will wander, people will begin to fidget and cough, and all the hard work you've put in will be lost as people will consider the speech boring.

If you stick to the seven-minute rule you will never be in the situation described above. No wedding speech should last longer than seven minutes; or, alternatively, you should be able to say everything you need to say in less than 1,000 words.

It's as simple as that: seven minutes or 1,000 words is my No. 1 tip for anyone who wants a speech that people remember.

KNOWING YOUR AUDIENCE

One of the most important pieces of advice that can be offered for any form of public speaking is to know your audience. 'But I already know the audience, I invited them', I hear you say. Yes, I know you did, but have you stopped to consider the average age, taste and upbringing of your guests? For example, Auntie Lil and friends might not take kindly to your recounting your first date which ended up with you both not leaving the bedroom for two days – for that matter, come to think of it, I don't think the father of the bride would be that chuffed either. Bear in mind the cross-section of people you are addressing, and try not to alienate anyone close to you.

DELIVERING YOUR SPEECH

The introduction is possibly the most important part of the speech, because you want to grab your guests' attention right from the start. So begin in a confident, slow and authoritative voice.

Treat the audience as one. A really good trick is to pretend that the audience (your guests) is just one person. When there's only one person that you have to worry about, you will feel more of a personal connection with them. Your speech will come second to the fact that you want to get your personal message across to that one person who is listening.

Make eye contact. Nothing will make your guests more alert and attentive. Don't deliver your speech with your head down, and your eyes glued to your prompt cards. Let your eyes wander from your notes and look around as often as possible.

Nearly everybody who is not trained in public speaking will speak too quickly. Slow yourself right down. You will need to practise this: speak at a pace that actually feels a little too slow at first; this is probably just about right.

Remember your words have to reach everybody in your venue. There may be a bit of an echo, and there's bound to be some background noise. Perhaps you are using a microphone, perhaps there are a few elderly guests who are hard of hearing – speaking slowly will help them hear what you have to say. Take breaths, pause between different parts of your speech. And refer to your prompt cards (see page 90).

STRUCTURE AND CONTENT

Your speech should flow and have a beginning, middle and an end. Perhaps begin with a humourous remark or anecdote about the day so far. This will really get the audience on your side from the start.

Thank the father of the bride

Thank the father of the bride for handing over to you and compliment him on his speech, even if it was a bad one. Make sure that you sound sincere!

Welcome everybody

So the bride's dad is on side, now for the rest of the room. Welcome everyone to the wedding and thank them for coming. Make a point of thanking the people who have travelled a long way to be there, perhaps from overseas.

Thank the bride's parents

Traditionally this is where you thank the bride's parents for giving you their daughter's hand in marriage, and welcoming you to their family. This can also be a good place for a joke, if you're going the funny route. Do make as much as possible of thanking the parents as they have probably paid for quite a lot of your wedding – not to mention the fact that it will make them feel good. You will also want to thank your own parents at this point. This is when you can present both mothers with a bouquet of flowers or other gift.

Absent friends

Should there be any close members of the family who could not attend the wedding because of illness, they should be mentioned and be wished a speedy recovery.

Special thanks and gifts

First, thank the people who have made the wedding and reception special. This could be anyone from the wedding planner to the bride's sister who helped with the flowers. Obviously your best man and ushers will also figure high on this list. Now is also a good time to present gifts to them. Fail to thank these people at your peril.

Say a few words about the bride

Once all the thank-you's are out of the way, it is time to say a few words about your new bride. It is always a good start to mention how lovely she looks, and to perhaps tell a story of how you met, or a funny anecdote. Although it's not tradition, you can ask everyone to raise a toast to the bride if you wish.

Propose a toast to the bridesmaids

Traditionally this is the groom's main task during his speech: to propose a toast to the bridesmaids on behalf of you and your new wife. Your toast may start with something like 'we admire them for their beauty, respect them for their intelligence, adore them for their virtues, and love them because we can't help it, please be upstanding and raise your glasses to . . . the bridesmaids!'

A few words about the best man

Finally, remember to thank the best man for coming as well as for arranging the stag do. You may want to recount some of the goings-on from the stag do, but check with the best man first – you don't

TOP TIP

These points may seem obvious, but believe, me plenty of grooms have tripped up on them!

Do	Don't
keep it personal	be embarrassing
make a joke or two	swear or use foul language
say what you want	talk just for the sake of it
thank all the people that helped	forget people's names
try to relax before your speech	get stinking drunk beforehand

want to steal the thunder from his speech. Present him with his thank-you gift. Now is a good time to make a joke about how the best man is soon to do his very best to blot your character, but not to believe a word of it etc. He's up next, so give him a good build-up! If you do not have a toastmaster, finish your speech by introducing and handing over to the best man.

PROMPT CARDS

If you are planning to memorise your speech and not necessarily having a full-length copy to hand, then creating some prompt cards is essential. These are small index cards on which you write the main points of your speech. Prompt cards keep you on track and give you confidence. They should read something like this:

Card 1   The opening line + welcome everyone
Card 2   Thank and compliment the father of bride
Card 3   Thank everyone for coming
Card 4   Thank bride's parents
Card 5   Absent friends

. . . You get the idea. These cards are just there to make sure that you don't forget people's names and where you are in your speech.

HOW TO DEAL WITH SPEECH NERVES

Nerves are caused by irrational fears, so what is the worst that could really happen? You might read your speech from your prompt cards and it might go a little flat. But remember, you're not a politician who has to cope with hecklers. Your audience are your friends and family and you have their good will. They've probably had a good bit to drink by now and will be feeling pretty merry.

Think of a funny story before you stand up. Nothing so funny that will have you crack up laughing and be unable to give your speech, but something that brings a smile to your face. Take a deep breath before you begin. Continue to breathe regularly. Don't go hyperventilating and making yourself feel faint, but concentrate on slowing your breathing down.

Remember that you have prompt cards to help keep you in check and on message.

SUBJECTS TO AVOID

There is nothing wrong with reciting funny or embarrassing stories about the best man, bride and, of course, your future mother-in-law, but you have to make sure that it is quite clear that any teasing is done with affection. You don't want to humiliate or upset; if in doubt, leave it out. Some subjects are obvious no-nos, however, it is amazing how many grooms and best men make the most obvious faux pas. Don't mention under any circumstances:

- **Ex-girlfriends.** Everyone knows that you have had past loves, but your bride does not want to be reminded on your wedding day. This is a sure-fire way to make the entire gathering squirm in their seats.
- **Divorce**. Talking about divorce at a wedding is similar to talking about death at the birth of a new child; you just don't do it.
- **Heavy drinking, drugs, gambling or fighting**. No good can come from any of these; however, don't be surprised if the best man alludes to one of these topics in his speech.
- **Arguments**. Arguments between you and your fiancée should be kept private. Your wedding day is a time to show how compatible you are, not dig up old frictions!
- **Unemployment or being fired**. Again, someone in the audience may be unemployed or may have just been fired; they do not need reminding of this.
- **Racist or homophobic jokes**. In bad taste at the best of times, but particularly inappropriate in a large gathering of people, where you may not know everyone closely.
- **Sexist jokes**. A little light banter about how you may become hen-pecked by your future wife is fine, but anything stronger won't go down well. Remember over half your audience will be female.
- **Womanising ways**. Don't imply that you have ever been a womaniser, even as a joke – even if you have been one in the past.

• **Brushes with the law.** Even if the best man is an ex-convict, he won't want everyone at the reception to know. Any skeletons in the cupboard are best left there.

IDEAS FOR YOUR SPEECH

On top of the essential components of your speech (as set out on pages 88–90) people are expecting funny anecdotes, perhaps about the proposal, your relationship and, of course, your stag do. You are not under the same pressure to make your audience laugh as the best man – a point never wasted when reminding the best man and everyone in the room during your own speech.

Opening lines

There is a saying that the old lines are the best, and they are not wrong. Keeping your opening line to a simple remark or quip is definitely the best way forward. It will get your audience on side, and help you to relax. Here are some opening lines guaranteed to bring a smile to even the stoniest face.

Good evening ladies and gentlemen. I have been told that this is one of the few times in a married man's life when he can be in the company of his wife and mother-in-law and not be interrupted . . . So I may be here some time.

I'd like to thank the Revd Grey for the great job he did today at the church. I learned something during the vows that I hadn't realised before: that it's OK to have sixteen wives: four better, four worse, four richer and four poorer. So I shall bear that in mind.

Good afternoon ladies and gentlemen. I must say, it's funny how history repeats itself. Twenty-four years ago, Anna's mum and dad were sending their beautiful daughter to bed with a dummy – and here we are again today.

I've heard a few people comment on how trim I am looking in this suit, which is actually the result of a fitness regime that's seen me do at least 50 push-ups a day during the run-up to this wedding. But I should mention that none of them have actually been intentional – I've just been collapsing a lot through nerves and stress.

I feel very fortunate to have married Anna. None of you will know this, but I've actually been congratulated already. 'Paul', my father said to me, 'Well done! You will always look back on today as the happiest and best thing you've ever done.' Fitting words, I thought, as I set off for my stag night.

Thank you for all your wonderful gifts. I can't tell you how much they mean to us, but I should have a better idea after the honeymoon, once I've spoken to the guy in the pawn shop.

Replying to the bride's father
I'd like to start by thanking Andrew for his kind words. I hope that, as Anna's husband, I can live up to the image he painted of me or, failing that, at least continue to keep pulling the wool over his eyes!

I'd like to thank Andrew for his kind and generous words. I'm hoping to be at least halfway to Italy by the time he realises that he's now married to a mother-in-law, and that it's my fault.

Thanking your own parents
There are two people not yet mentioned, but without whom I wouldn't be here. No, I don't mean the best man and the taxi driver, but my parents, the most wonderful mum and dad in the world.

Observations about the wedding
It is always a nice thing to include some comments about the wedding in your speech, from comments on the decor of the venue to the food, which has hopefully been delicious, and having all your friends round you. As I've said before, making your speech up on the day is a cardinal sin, but obviously specific remarks will have to be improvised on the day. General observations could be:

Anna has to be congratulated for organising today. I'm not saying I didn't do my bit, I am here after all, but I'm sure you'll all agree she's done a fantastic job. I hope that every day will be as happy as today . . . and considerably less expensive.

I must say it has been a wonderful day and a very emotional wedding for both of us – even the cake is in tiers.

The early days of your relationship
Anna and I met in a very, very romantic location: the Hippodrome nightclub in Exeter. This place is renowned for being the hang-out of drunk wide boys and white stiletto girls, so it was pure coincidence that we met on that fateful night.

I should have realised the first time I met Anna what I was letting myself in for. Not only did she insist on buying the drinks, she drove me home, told me to phone her, told me when to phone her, then gave me a full account of what she expected me to say when I did phone her. Well, apparently, I've always enjoyed a bit of domination.

Describe how the romance developed
Anna and I began our relationship like many young lovebirds, by spending almost every moment together – during which time Anna tried to decide if she could do any better.

When Anna finally agreed to go out with me, to try and impress her, I took her out to a really fancy restaurant. And the evening went well; I made her laugh so hard . . . she dropped her fries.

Describe what you've learned from each other
Since I started going out with Anna I have really started to go places. It was 'to the bar' when I first met her, 'to get on my bike' when I grew a moustache, 'to the florist's' when I forgot Valentine's Day, and, of course, when I proposed . . . to her parents' house for permission. And I'm delighted that they gave it!

Anna, I thank you for turning up at the church today. You might wonder why I should be grateful to Anna for marrying me. It's because she's been such a good influence on me already, and I feel I've become a better person for knowing her and I'll become an even better person for marrying her. If you think how good I am now, just think how brilliant I'll be in a couple of years!

Say why you think you are so well suited

I think we complement each other very well. Anna is ambitious, industrious, highly motivated and loves a challenge. And I am that challenge.

Anna and I are very well suited to each other; clearly, I am the boss in the relationship, whilst Anna is just the decision-maker.

Provide an amusing insight into your relationship

Most couples have their funny stories, and while some of these should remain private, the odd anecdote always goes down a blast:

I'll never forget the time I surprised Anna with some lingerie . . . she'd never seen me wearing anything in red before!

Living with Anna has been great. We are a real team. I do all the painting and decorating and Anna does all the cooking and cleaning. Then we try to guess what I've painted and what Anna's cooked.

Compliment your bride

Don't under any circumstances, none whatsoever, forget to pay some personal and heartfelt compliments to your bride:

When it comes to talking about my bride's good points, where do I start? She's intelligent, generous, hard-working, popular and a brilliant judge of character.

I think you'll agree that Anna looks stunning in that magnificent white dress. I feel so proud and honoured to be married to her. And of course, I can at last say: my dishwasher matches my fridge!

Anna is beautiful. She's intelligent. She's funny. She can cook like Nigella Lawson and she's got the patience of a saint. I can say with my hand on my heart that I'm one of the luckiest men alive. And she writes a cracking bridegroom's speech as well.

I had no idea such a wonderful combination of qualities could exist in one person, until I met my wife. Anna, you are everything I never knew I wanted.

Say how happy and fortunate you are

Many people have told me how lucky I am to be marrying Anna, including Anna. And they are right.

To my wife, my bride and joy, thank you for everything you have done. You know everything about me and love me just the same. I have my faults, yet you still agreed to marry me. I am extremely lucky today to be the one to marry you – and I hope this is the start of many happy years together.

Closing your speech

I will shortly be handing over to Jason. But unlike many best man speeches, which are full of sexual innuendo, he has promised me that if there is anything slightly risqué, he will whip it out immediately.

USING QUOTATIONS

Look up the words 'love' and 'marriage' in any dictionary of quotations, and you'll find thousands of entries. They can add some poignancy to your speech, particularly if you elaborate on why it is so meaningful and relevant to you both. Here is just a tiny selection.

The goal in marriage is not to think alike, but to think together.

Robert C. Dodds

Happy marriages begin when we marry the ones we love, and they blossom when we love the ones we marry.

Tom Mullen

Chains do not hold a marriage together. It is threads, hundreds of tiny threads which sew people together through the years. That is what makes a marriage last – more than passion or even sex!

Simone Signoret

Getting a dog is like getting married. It teaches you to be less self-centred, to accept sudden, surprising outbursts of affection, and not to be upset by a few scratches on your car.

W. H. Auden

To keep your marriage brimming / With love in the wedding cup,
Whenever you're wrong, admit it; / Whenever you're right, shut up.

Ogden Nash

I love being married. It's so great to find that one special person you want to annoy for the rest of your life.

Rita Rudner

Compromise: An amiable arrangement between husband and wife whereby they agree to let her have her own way.

Anon.

Marriage requires a person to prepare four types of 'rings': engagement ring wedding ring, suffering and enduring.

Anon.

A successful marriage requires falling in love many times, always with the same person.

Germaine Greer

To love someone deeply gives you strength. Being loved by someone deeply gives you courage.

Lao Tzu

CHAPTER 11

THE HONEYMOON

Choosing your honeymoon has got to be one of the most exciting parts of all your marriage preparations. With so many exotic and exciting places to visit, the choice almost seems too much. The honeymoon is an excuse to have a once-in-a-lifetime holiday to the destination of your dreams. But don't necessarily follow other people's preconceived ideas about the sort of place you should go. Whatever makes the two of you happy will make it romantic. The most important thing is that you are together. Your honeymoon is a vitally important way for you both to relax after the wedding, alone at last.

You have both probably been sharing ideas on your honeymoon since the day you were engaged. A successful honeymoon trip is more than a holiday, it is the start of your married life together.

A fun way to start planning your honeymoon is to both go out separately and get as many holiday brochures as you can. Once you are both home, lay them out across the table, grab a bottle of wine and start planning your dream honeymoon.

Traditionally, however, the groom plans the honeymoon as a complete surprise for his bride. So, perhaps after sounding out your fiancée's initial ideas, you look after this one by yourself. After all, she's probably got more than enough on her plate with all the other wedding arrangements.

WHAT SORT OF HONEYMOON?

Make sure you both want the same things out of your honeymoon. There is little point in going to an excessively hot destination such as India if your fiancée cannot tolerate the sun. Likewise, if your future wife has a phobia of, say, crowds, then a place such as Morocco, where the markets and the medina are often crowded, hot and stuffy, is a no-go area.

It's probably a good idea to go somewhere you have both never been before. What sort of honeymoon do you want? While you're feeling exhausted from all the planning of your wedding, the idea of doing nothing but lazing on a beach may sound, quite literally, like paradise. But, if you're going to be stranded on a tropical island for three weeks, be sure that this is really what you want to do. Perhaps you want to consider booking some activities – such as windsurfing or scuba-diving.

Make sure that neither of you feels pressured by the other into doing something you are not really keen on. Since opposites often attract, this may be reflected in your ideas of the perfect honeymoon. This is where dual-centre holidays can be the solution. You can thus combine relaxing on the beach with more active alternatives, or even just city sightseeing. Kenya is an ideal dual-centre destination. You can go on a breathtaking African safari for the first half of the honeymoon, then relax on the stunning Indian Ocean beaches for the second half.

If you are both pretty adventurous, a South American honeymoon is one to consider – offering you treks through the Andes. Or if art and culture is your thing, then how about Florence, Venice or Paris – perennial favourites with honeymooning couples, and still wonderfully romantic. There are some really wonderful British hotels, so you could consider remaining on home ground.

Make a list of each of your dream destinations, then compare them and see how similar they are. The world really is your oyster.

HOW LONG?

Once you have agreed on the right sort of honeymoon, work out how long you would like to go for – the longer the better, presumably! Most honeymoons last for 14 nights, but this is by no means a fixed time. You could go for 21 days or even a month – ultimately it comes down to the amount of time that both of you are able to get off work.

Many employers have a company policy of not allowing employees to take more than two weeks' consecutive holiday at once, but talk to them. Since it's for your honeymoon, they may well be prepared to bend this rule, especially if they are given plenty of notice and can perhaps arrange cover for you.

When do you want to travel? Do you want to leave the morning after your wedding or do you want to have some time to unwind and pack when you'll be able to think about it a bit more? These are all questions that need to be answered before paying out a great deal of money on your dream honeymoon.

THE BUDGET

You should already have allocated an amount to spend on your honeymoon when you and your fiancée worked out the overall budget for your wedding. Long-haul destinations aren't as expensive as they used to be. There are good deals to be had, if you do your research carefully. We are all now so accustomed to making travel arrangements via the Internet, that you could easily overlook your high-street travel agent. You could be surprised at where the best deal will come from.

Of course, you don't want to break the bank, but there are some areas where it's really not worth scrimping. It's those extra special, luxurious touches that can make the difference. So perhaps consider staying in the UK and Europe, but going all out on the five-star treatment. The more of your honeymoon budget you spend on flights, the less you have to spend on what you do and where you stay when you get there. If going further afield, look at all-inclusive, full-board packages or resorts. That way you won't need to set aside quite so much spending money.

TOP TIP

I usually advise couples to exercise extreme caution when putting any substantial wedding costs on their credit cards. The interest rates can be crippling. So only take up the following suggestion if sure you are able to pay off the credit card, as you do not want to start married life overwhelmingly in debt. Consider paying your wedding suppliers and venue with a credit card that allocates you points which can be used in conjunction with a travel agent or web site. Look at your existing credit cards. Perhaps you've already got thousands of air miles accumulated there that you can put towards your honeymoon.

WHEN TO GO WHERE

There's little point in visiting your dream destination only to find that the small print in the holiday brochure forgot to mention that it is rainy season. For example, the wedding season in the UK runs from April through to September, but this is rainy season in the Maldives, which just happens to be one of the most popular honeymoon destinations in the world. So it pays to do a little research on your chosen honeymoon destination. To give you an idea, here are some of the top honeymoon destinations' high seasons, according to month.

December–March	April–July	August–November
Caribbean	Caribbean	Europe
Mexico	Australia	Aruba
Costa Rica	Florida	Canada
Maldives	Europe	USA
Asia	Thailand	Dubai

Try to book your honeymoon as soon as possible. Some couples even set their wedding date around their honeymoon if there's a specific place they've always wanted to visit.

THE TOP 10 HONEYMOON DESTINATIONS OF 2006

1. Sri Lanka. This tropical teardrop island at the foot of India has some of the most spectacular and beautiful scenery in the world. The beautiful golden sand of the palm-fringed beaches offer an ideal place to relax, and the local history and culture provide some breathtaking sights.

2. St Lucia. St Lucia is an island of amazing natural beauty, offering many diverse attractions to inspire and fulfil, arousing your senses and leaving you with many happy memories. Its most famous and breathtaking sight has to be the Pitons in the south-west: twin volcanic peaks rising majestically and dramatically from the water.

3. USA. Selecting an American honeymoon means options that stretch, literally, from sea to shining sea. Whether the two of you would like the mountain beauty of Colorado, the beach fun of California, Hawaii or Florida, the big city excitement of New York, the cosy charm of New England or the outdoor adventure found throughout the nation, you'll find many tempting choices.

4. Mauritius. This is the Garden of Eden, 'the original paradise, amid scenes as beautiful as the hand of God ever created.' Many a traveller before you, from ancient mariners and merchants to modern astronauts and business people have been seduced by the tantalising beauty of the colours and costumes of this land.

5. Antigua. Antigua is one of the Leeward Islands and boasts a choice of 365 picturesque coves and palm-fringed bays, with fine sand, blue seas and some of the best water sports in the Caribbean.

6. Barbados. Barbados has a wonderful climate, great beaches and a variety of good quality restaurants and bars as well as lively nightlife in the south of the island. Barbados is the most easterly island in the Caribbean chain and, as a former British colony, it retains many familiar characteristics.

7. Mexico. Mexico is a traveller's paradise, crammed with a multitude of opposing identities: desert landscapes, snow-capped volcanoes, ancient ruins, teeming industrialised cities, time-warped colonial towns, glitzy resorts, lonely beaches.

8. Jamaica. The capital is Kingston, situated on the south coast. If the island is mostly an exotic paradise of sighing breezes, swaying palms and turquoise seas, not so its capital, which is neither pretty nor charming but everything you would expect a busy Caribbean port city to be: crowded, lively and, occasionally, even aggressive.

9. Kenya. Kenya offers the traveller a land richly endowed by nature with what some consider to be the most exciting wildlife in the world, along with stunning tropical shores lapped by the warm waters of the Indian Ocean.

TOP TIPS

Take into consideration costs and time. A direct, non-stop flight may be a bit more expensive than a flight involving lay-overs, but it will be more convenient and eliminates reboarding troubles. Remember that most charter flights are 'no frills'. So if you are looking for something beyond the basics, you will need to avoid a charter flight. There are some really great deals to be had on business and first-class lounges at most departure airports in the UK, so why not treat yourselves to a little luxury before you board the plane?.

10. Thailand. From the bustling capital of Bangkok to the northern retreats of Chiang Mai, Chiang Rai and Mae Hong Sorn, Thailand boasts a spectacular array of glittering temples and huge Buddhist statues, saffron-robed monks and fascinating hill tribes.

TRAVEL INSURANCE

It never ceases to amaze me how many people travel abroad without travel insurance, when in every case the small cost of the insurance far outweighs the peace of mind that it brings. The costs of medical treatment abroad can be excessive – it can certainly eat up all your honeymoon spending money, and beyond. Take the USA for instance: you cannot even be seen in a hospital unless you have proof of travel insurance or a valid credit card. With a simple broken arm costing upwards of $7,000, all of a sudden the £39-per-person cost of travel insurance doesn't seem that much.

INOCULATIONS AND VISAS

As we all travel further and further across the world to far-flung destinations, it is always worth remembering that some of these countries carry diseases with which we do not normally come into contact. Always check with your doctor or district nurse which, if any, inoculations are needed to travel to your chosen destination.

Over the past 10 years, there has been great controversy over all the different types of malaria tablets available and over which ones are the most effective. (It is worth noting that some malaria medication does have extreme side effects in some cases.) If you are travelling to a malaria-infected area, then do not, under any circumstances, consider not taking the prescribed medication. Getting malaria on your honeymoon will far outweigh any side effects the pills may have.

Before booking your honeymoon, always check whether you need any special visas or documentation to travel to that country. Some countries require you to visit their embassy and pay hefty fees to obtain a visa.

HEADING OFF ON HONEYMOON

If you have arranged your honeymoon as a surprise for your bride, then make sure you have told her in plenty of time what sort of clothes she will need to bring. She may want to go out and invest in a few new bikinis. Don't forget to check that both your passports are in date.

In the week before your honeymoon, you will want to confirm all your travel arrangements. If, like most couples, you are heading off on your honeymoon straight from your wedding-night hotel, you have the added stress of having to remember everything else associated with honeymoons and holidays. Here is a quick checklist of things to make sure you have organised before you set off for your wedding:

• **Passports and visas**. It is always a good idea to put one of you in charge of holding the passports from the start as this will avoid the argument at the airport of 'I thought you had the passports!'
• **Currency**. Have your money changed at least a week before your wedding day. Travellers' cheques are the safest way to carry large amounts of foreign currency, but it is always a good idea to have some local currency ready for tips at the airport and hotel.
• **Pack and check**. Sounds silly, but so many grooms forget to pack things such as shorts or T-shirts, so lay out all of your clothes on the bed and make sure that you have everything that you might need. Remember that weight is a factor as most airlines are very strict on overweight baggage – check with your airline for restrictions.
• **First-aid kit**. Always carry one just in case of small cuts or sunburn, etc.

TOP TIP

Why not ask your best men to arrange to get your honeymoon luggage delivered to your wedding-night hotel prior to the wedding itself – that way you will not need to worry about it at all on the day. Make sure those passports and travel documents are somewhere safe.

APPENDICES

COMPLETE WEDDING COUNTDOWN
At least six months before . . .

- Buy an engagement ring – if you haven't already! Custom says it should cost at least a month's salary. Don't forget to insure it.
- Agree on a wedding date, time and location.
- Decide which kind of ceremony you want: religious or civil.
- Choose your religious or civil venue, and book in your service with whomever the officiator will be (priest, rabbi, Registrar, etc).
- Agree on a style and theme for the ceremony, including music.
- Book a band and/or DJ.
- Arrange for the marriage license.
- Agree on the number of guests to attend the ceremony and draft a guest list.
- Agree on the number of guests to attend the reception and draft a guest list.
- Decide on and book a reception venue.
- Agree on a budget and decide who is going to pay for what. The days where the father of the bride foots the bill are over by the way; these days it's usually a joint effort. See pages 112-113 for details.
- Agree on a style and theme for the reception.
- Arrange for a tent or a marquee, if required.
- Hire a caterer for the reception and agree on a menu.
- Think about the style and flavour of the wedding cake, find a cake maker and order it.
- Choose your wedding rings.
- Choose the best man and the ushers. When choosing the best man, think carefully. Don't just choose the funniest friend you have, as making a funny speech will be just one of his many responsibilities. Choose someone who can rise to the huge challenge of being your right-hand man until – and on – the big day.
- Decide on whether you will have any readings at the ceremony and if so, who will perform them.
- Think about formalwear for the best man and ushers. Arrange for the hire of formalwear, if required. Enlist the help of the best man.

- Book a tailor, if required.
- Book a photographer and videographer, if required.
- Book transportation for the wedding day.
- Book a room at your first-night hotel, if required.
- Decide on a honeymoon destination and book the transportation and accommodation. Remember to buy travel insurance.
- Compile a wedding list together and place it in your desired shop(s). Make sure the shop(s) know to send your gifts to you after you return from the honeymoon.
- Consider a pre-nuptial agreement.

Three months before . . .

- Choose and order the invitations/response cards and make sure they are sent out a minimum of six weeks prior to the day. Make sure to mention the type of dress you want, ie. black tie.
- Prepare map/accommodation details, if required, and send out together with the invitations.
- Establish a method of tracking acceptances and refusals as your guests reply.
- Choose and order place cards for the tables.
- Discuss the ceremony/service with the priest/rabbi/Registrar.
- Confirm band/DJ.
- Finalise the ceremony and reception guest lists. Tell as many invitees as you can to save the date.
- Create wedding Web page. Be sure to include details of the ceremony, reception, travel and accommodation.
- Attend a clothes fitting. Make sure your groomsmen do the same.
- Order the wedding rings. Don't forget to take out insurance.
- Confirm that your passports are up to date.
- Obtain all necessary visas and organise innoculations, if the ceremony and/or honeymoon location requires them.
- Make sure the best man is thinking about your stag weekend, including a date (make sure it's at least a week before the wedding!), venue, location and invitee list.

One month before . . .

- Buy wedding gifts for your bride and the attendants; it is traditional to buy her a gift, no matter how much you've already spent on the wedding.
- Pick up the wedding rings. Make sure they fit, and guard them with your life.
- Inform the reception venue and caterers of the final number of guests.
- Prepare a seating plan for the reception.
- Meet with photographer/videographer to finalise arrangements.
- Inform band/DJ of any song requests. Choose a first-dance song.
- Make sure all legal documents are in order – note that this area falls firmly into the realm of your responsibilities.
- Confirm honeymoon arrangements. Prove what a thoughtful husband you will be by arranging to have the honeymoon suite filled with champagne, strawberries and your bride's favourite flowers (ask her sister/bridesmaid!).
- Make sure you know where you'll be staying on your wedding night. Most couples now spend at least one night near the wedding venue before jetting off on their honeymoon.
- Make appointments to get yourself spruced up just before the wedding – nose hair and wedding photos do not mix.
- Confirm all on-the-day arrangements (catering, drinks, flowers, guest accommodation, etc) with all the suppliers. Imagine a wedding without music, or a cake, or someone to marry you . . . Pay down anything you can early – there will be many bills to come.
- Double check that the best man is doing his job – ask for updates!
- Take delivery of airline tickets. Put them somewhere you won't lose them, along with your passports.
- Arrange a time for the wedding rehearsal.
- You'll probably be having your stag party around now. Enjoy!

One week before . . .

- Pick up (and try on) outfits and check you have all the necessary accessories: cufflinks, kilt socks, full hip flask in case she's really late.
- Ask the best man to arrange for your wedding clothes to be collected from first-night hotel and stored or returned to the hire shop.
- Pack for the night after the wedding and for the honeymoon.
- Help the bride with all those delightful last-minute tasks such as assembling favours boxes and picking up her relatives from the airport.
- Make sure your best man and ushers know what to do on the day – ask Google rather than a preoccupied bride-to-be if you're not sure.
- Get spending money together for the honeymoon – yes, you must pay for that too. Never mind, at least you put spanking new luggage on the gift list . . .
- Make yourself look nice with a haircut – you could even push the boat out and get a facial and manicure if you're comfortable with being a modern man.
- Start writing your speech. Practice it! (See pages 114-122 for sample speeches.)
- Make sure the best man is working on his speech. Beware hastily written and off-the-cuff speeches – they can bomb horribly.
- Make a detailed timetable for your wedding day. Give a copy to the best man.
- Hold rehearsal with bride, groom, bride's father, best man, bridesmaids, flower girls, page boys and ushers.
- Advise best man of the seating plan at the ceremony. He will tell the ushers.
- Do a final check on your honeymoon plans and do any last-minute shopping.

One day before . . .

- Make sure you have all the messages to be read out at the reception.
- Give the wedding rings to your best man. Watch him sweat.
- Arrange for the delivery of the cake to the venue.
- Make sure the going-away transportation will be in the right place at the right time.
- Try to relax, limit yourself to one stiff drink only and have an early night.

BUDGET PLANNER

This budget planner is designed to help you keep track of the various – and numerous – costs of your wedding, so that you don't overspend. It is also a rough guide to who pays for what, although these days there is greater flexibility over financial responsibility.

Wedding	Who Pays	Budget	Deposit	Actual Cost
Announcements	Bride's family			
Engagement party	Bride's family			
Registrar/church fees	Groom			
Ceremony venue fee	Groom			
Marriage certificate	Groom			
Choir/music	Bride's family			
Ceremony and reception flowers and decorations	Bride's family			
Bouquets & buttonholes	Groom			
Stationery & postage	Bride's family			
Reception venue	Bride's family			
Reception flowers	Bride's family			
Reception food	Bride's family			
Reception drinks	Bride's family			
Cake	Bride's family			
Entertainment	Bride's family			
Photographer and prints	Bride's family			
Videographer	Bride's family			
Gifts for wedding party	Bride/groom			
The seating plan chart (if done professionally)	Bride's family			
Car hire for the bridal party on the wedding day	Bride's family			
Tips for all services	Bride's family`			
				TOTAL:

...ngs	Who Pays	Budget	Deposit	Actual Cost
...ide's engagement ring	Groom			
...ide's wedding ring	Groom			
...room's wedding ring	Bride			
			TOTAL :	

...othing & beauty	Who Pays	Budget	Deposit	Actual Cost
...ide's wedding dress, ...oes and accessories	Bride's family			
...akeup and hair trial ...d on the day	Bride			
...room's suit and accessories	Groom's family			
...idesmaids' dresses ...d accessories	Bridesmaids			
...st man's suit and accessories	Best man			
...shers' suits and accessories	Ushers			
...ower girls' dresses	Bride's family			
...ge boys' suits and accessories	Bride's family			
			TOTAL:	

...neymoon	Who Pays	Budget	Deposit	Actual Cost
...oing-away transport	Groom			
...rst-night accommodation	Groom			
...oneymoon accommodation	Groom			
...ending money	Bride/groom			
			TOTAL:	
			GRAND TOTAL:	

SAMPLE SPEECHES

These sample speeches are just that – samples. They are not here for you to copy out word for word and recite parrot fashion! They are just here as a starting point, to help you write your own speech, a skeleton that you can flesh out with your own personal touches. Perhaps some parts are definitely not right for you, perhaps you can select bits to adapt. Indeed, some of these speeches share some components, but mixed in with different text – to show you how you can achieve different tones with the same basic structure.

SPEECH 1

Reverend, Ladies and Gentlemen, [pause] Thank you very much, George, for those kind words. It goes almost without saying how pleased I am to be here today. In order not to dull your pleasure I intend to only speak for a few minutes in case we all get snowed in!

As you all know Helen has been a much sought-after woman, but I'm pleased to announce the winner of the competition, me. There are no runners up, or consolation prizes.

My new mother-in-law, Claire, has worked long and hard for many months to prepare this wonderful occasion. All the little details such as these beautiful flower/cake decorations were planned by her, and my father-in-law has taken on his second mortgage without complaint, like the good-natured man he is. I am very pleased to be part of the family and know that my parents feel the same.

Speaking of whom, today represents a great occasion for both my parents, being the culmination of many years of planning of a different sort. They have prepared me well, supported me through school and university and taught me the difference between right and wrong, so that I know which I am enjoying at any given time!

I would like to thank you all for your presence in both senses of the word, but especially for the smiling faces I see in front of me. I am particularly pleased that Aunt Alice managed to make the long journey from New York for this occasion, and we are all delighted that Helen's sister flew all the way from Washington to join us and to be such a charming bridesmaid. Of course she had a 'little help' – quite a big help, actually, from Maggie, who looked so sweet holding Helen's train.

My best man, Robert, has made everything go smoothly and made his contribution to what has seemed the perfect day.

Finally, I must pay tribute to the bridesmaids, whose invaluable support has helped to make this day so successful.

In conclusion, thank you, everybody, for listening, and I hope you are having a wonderful evening and are all as happy as we are today. Would you kindly stand and raise your glasses and drink a toast to the health of your hosts, two wonderful people, Clare and George. [Pause] To Clare and George!

And now I hand you over to Robert, my best man.

SPEECH 2

Ladies and Gentlemen, until today, 21 April has not been a very historic day: I was hoping to give you all a short list of fascinating events that had happened 'On this day in History,' but not much has happened: a quick look on The History Channel.com told me that on this day in 1918 the Red Baron was killed in action over France; in 1926 Queen Elizabeth II was born; and on this day in the year 2001, you attended this wedding reception and heard the finest wedding speech of your entire lifetime, and my best man, Andrew, will be making it.

I did, of course, have a great speech of my own worked out for you today, but as I am now married, my wife has told me what to say instead.

Anyway, thank you Michael for those kind words, I am proud to be your son-in-law; I hope I can live up to your expectations. I would sincerely like to thank you and Jackie for always making me feel very welcome when I come to visit, and for giving us this wonderful wedding and reception. Most of all, thank you for giving me your blessing to marry your lovely daughter, Erica.

Thank you for all the help with today's preparations, the flowers, the favours, the limos, the finance – the list is endless. I must also thank Michael and Jackie for bringing up such a lovely daughter. In addition, due to the number of phone calls between Erica and her mother, the phone company would also like to thank you both.

Today also represents a great occasion for both my parents, being the culmination of many years of planning of a different sort. They have prepared me well, supported me through school and university and taught me the difference between right and wrong, but only so that I know which I am enjoying at any given time! Thank you for your love and support over the years, for all the advice you have given us, for putting up with us and pointing us in the right direction.

As for the rest of you, on behalf on my wife and I, we would like to thank all of you for coming here today and sharing our special day with us. Especially those who have travelled so far to be here.

I would like to thank you all for your presence in both senses of the word, it's been like Christmas every day for about a month now. It will be hard to come home to find just the usual bills and junk mail from now on. But a huge thank you for all the presents and for your cards and kind thoughts, but most of all for the smiling faces I see in front of me.

I asked Rachel, Erica's chief bridesmaid, a few weeks ago how Erica looks in her wedding dress; she said that she looked wonderful, but that didn't prepare me enough for when I saw her walk down the aisle. I was overwhelmed to the say the least by how beautiful Erica looks today.

I want everyone here, especially Erica, to know how lucky I feel to be here right now. Erica is beautiful, intelligent, hard-working. The list of her qualities is extremely long. But, unfortunately I can't read her handwriting – must be something to do with her being a doctor.

But seriously, to my wife, my bride and joy, thank you for

everything you have done. You know everything about me and love me just the same. I have my faults, yet you still agreed to marry me. I am extremely lucky today to be the one to marry you – and I hope this is the start of many happy years together.

We have been planning this wedding for over a year now, although it seems like a lifetime. Well, I say 'we', really Erica did all the work, I just agreed to show up on the day! So a big thank you to all that have helped us, but especially to Erica who has managed so well.

A special thank you to John Taylor, (my flat mate at university) who could not be here today, but who is responsible for introducing Erica and I way back in 1994.

I would like to thank Andrew for agreeing to be my best man. He has been a tower of strength throughout the proceedings. Well, that is to say he was there when we picked out the tuxes. Haven't seen much of him since. Of course the trouble with being the best man at a wedding is that you never get to prove it.

Erica and I would also like to thank James and Andy for being ushers today. James asked one guest today if she was a 'friend of the groom' to which she replied, 'Certainly not, I'm the bride's mother!'. Only joking, Jackie! But here's a special 'thank you' to Andy for agreeing to be my usher and for doing such a fine job considering the appalling job Dave and I did at his wedding.

A final and big 'thank you' goes to our bridesmaids: Rachel, Jenny and Laura. Laura could not be here today as she was giving birth to a 10 and a half pound baby boy – I don't know, the excuses people will come up with not to attend your wedding! – but 10 and a half pounds is a lot of baby! Let's raise a glass to Laura! To Rachel and Jen, we would like to say how lovely you look and thank you for doing such a wonderful job today. Ladies and Gentlemen, please be upstanding. I would like to propose a toast to the bridesmaids.

Well I could stand here and give you a load of stale old jokes, but instead I think I'll leave that to the best man. Ladies and gentlemen, Mr Andrew Simpson!

SPEECH 3

Thanks Neil, and thanks for your generosity in providing such a splendid reception and, as a Manchester United supporter, missing out on watching today's FA Cup Final! I'm not good at speeches, so I'll try to keep to less than half an hour . . .

Both Allison and I would like to say a big 'thank you' to everyone for being here today and sharing this special occasion with us, and I know many of you have travelled a long way to be here, so we hope you really enjoy the day. Thank you all very much for all your many cards and presents which are very much appreciated. Some family and friends haven't been able to make it here today, owing to imminent new arrivals amongst other things, so they're in our thoughts as I'm sure we're in theirs.

Neil and Jill, thank you very much for your support and for welcoming me into your family, and thank you both for this lovely reception. I am really proud to have become Allison's husband, and in the process, your son-in-law. I promise I'll take good care of her.

I would also like to thank my own parents for their love, support and patience through the years of loud music, guitars and motorbikes, which I'm sure I'll grow out of one day. Thank you for a great start in life and for your contribution to today's event.

And now I think we have some flowers for two very special mothers . . .

So to my wife. It doesn't seem five minutes since I was proposing to Allison under the stars and, as it was a freezing cold night, I ensured she had to answer 'yes' quickly before she could get back in the car to warm up. I'm so glad I'm married to Allison . . . caring, talented, modest, good-looking . . . I can see why you picked me.

Seriously though, the term 'better half' doesn't quite do you justice. I suppose every groom thinks his bride is the most beautiful in the world and that's how I feel today. I'm completely overwhelmed at how fantastic she looks and feel hugely privileged that she's chosen to be my wife. I commented before the wedding that, in my nervous state I probably wouldn't notice what she was wearing, but there was absolutely no danger of that happening. Thank you for making this the best day of my life and I hope that every day will be as happy as today . . . just less expensive.

I would like to give big thanks for a job well done, to my aptly named 'best man', Ken. My long-time school friend and a 'great, really, really nice bloke' . . . who would never say anything embarrassing about me in his speech . . . Let me assure you in advance that all the good stuff's true but anything else is pure fiction.

We would also like to thank Clare for being an excellent bridesmaid. You've been terrific and I'm sure you all agree that she too looks beautiful. Thanks for helping Allison with her preparations today and in the past months. So, in traditional fashion, would you please be upstanding as I propose a toast. To the bridesmaid!

And we have a small token of our appreciation here, for both Clare and Ken . . .

Allison and I will be holding an 'open house' tomorrow between 12 and 3, if anyone would like to pop round for a drink and view the presents – if we can unwrap them all in time! Speak to us later if you need directions . . . Lastly, I read somewhere that 'a man is incomplete until he is married . . . after that he is finished.' Which is what I am now, so again, thank you all for coming and I'll hand over to Ken.

SPEECH 4

Thank you David – although it's a bit late to warn me about your daughter's cooking skills. I would sincerely like to thank you and

Pam for giving us this wonderful wedding and reception. Also, for giving your blessing for me to marry your lovely daughter, Linda.

I would also like to thank my parents for their contribution towards the wedding, and also for giving me a very happy upbringing and a very happy family life. The only two things I won't miss are my Mum's baking and my Dad's jokes. Mum said to me the other day, I've baked some assorted cakes, do you want to take your pick? I said no, my hammer and chisel should do. Mind you, I'll say one thing for Mum, she puts up with Dad's jokes; in fact she knows all his jokes backwards. Unfortunately, she usually tells them that way.

Dad came out on the stag night, and he really enjoyed himself. He even did a spot of dancing down at the nightclub. A woman said to me 'Who's that man with the grey hair?' I said, 'It's my dad.' I thought, blimey, he's pulled, so I said to her, 'What do you think of the way he moves?' She said, 'Not a lot, he dances like an MFI wardrobe.'

Linda and I would like to thank you all very much for your cards, kind thoughts and wonderful presents. I would also like to say how overwhelmed I am by how beautiful Linda looks in her wedding dress; and also how lovely the bridesmaids look. If Julie and Anita would like to come out here, we would like to give them a small gift as a token of our thanks, and as a memento of this lovely day. Ladies and gentleman, please be upstanding, I would like to propose a toast to the bridesmaids.

I would also like to thank Tom and Brian for being such helpful ushers. Last but not least, I would like to thank my best man, Craig. He has been a tower of strength throughout the proceedings. I can't get over how well he has scrubbed up. Any of you that know Craig will know that he usually looks as if he has dressed in front of an aeroplane propeller. Mind you, I'll say one thing for him, he always has a bath once a week. Whether he needs it or not!

Anyway, I'm not going to stand here and give you all a load of stale old jokes, but I'm going to hand you over to somebody who will. Ladies and Gentlemen, the best man, Craig.

SPEECH 5

You don't always get a chance to tell people the things you feel most strongly. But you can do it at a wedding, and I'm glad to have the chance. I know a few of you think I took my time to get around to this, but let's be realistic – I'm a methodical guy. You can't rush the important things, and so I didn't. I waited for the perfect wife, and the perfect moment. And don't say I don't stick to my guns once my mind's made up, because technically speaking, I probably shouldn't be here today. At least, not if you believe this 'Test Your Stress Level' guide I found the other day. Count along with me while we take the test now.

1. Is your favourite team performing below their best at present? If so, give yourself 10 points.
2. Are you getting married in the next twelve months? 25 points.
3. If you are getting married, will you or your partner be involved in organising the wedding? If yes, add another 40.
4. Are things getting a bit tricky at work? If yes, add another 50.

Well, there were a few more like that, and it turns out I score so high I'm basically a ticking bomb. But even so, once I've made my mind up, wild horses wouldn't hold me back, and here I am – and glad to be here.

Jill – in case any of you hadn't noticed – is the perfect wife, and I'm lucky she said yes. I'm lucky to have someone who can live with my singing. I'm lucky to have someone who can live with my bad jokes. And I'm lucky to have someone who is just so good hearted and so lovely to be with.

Someone once said laughter is the shortest distance between two people. Well, Jill and I laugh together all the time, and that means a lot, I think.

All in all, I feel pretty good today! And I have to say it's pretty good to see you all here too. So thank you all for coming as far as many of you had to; thank you for the kind gifts; thank you for all the good wishes; and thank you, George, for deciding even at this late stage to turf out the embarrassing stuff from your speech.

Most of all, though, there are some special thanks I want to make. Mum and Dad, I want to thank you for everything. And that's saying a lot. Whenever I've needed anything, you've been there. Whenever we needed to talk, you've been just a phone call away. And when things have got tough, you've always been there to help, no matter what. You're the best.

This is the first time that I can truly say that all my friends and family and everyone who is dear to me has come together in one place and it's a great sight to see. Moments like this remind you that it's your family and friends who matter most. The material things are fun, but they're not what really matters when you come down to it. It's the love and support of the people in your life that mean everything to you. So thank you all for everything you've done to make this day possible.

And I especially want to thank you, Alex and Claire, for helping to organise today. Of course, from today I officially have a mother-in-law, and in the comedians' book of gags, that means I have years of misery to look forward to. But I don't accept a word of that. I have a glamorous mother-in-law who's every bit as beautiful as her daughter. All in all, my life right now is perfect. And on that note, I'll say thank you, cheers, and have a great time, everyone!

USEFUL RESOURCES

As you know by now, there is a great deal involved in planning a wedding. Listed here are some sources of essential information, plus suppliers, to get you started. Good luck, and happy planning!

Civil ceremonies

British Humanist Society   www.humanism.org.uk
General Register Office   www.gro.gov.uk
General Register Office for Scotland   www.gro-scotland.gov.uk
General Register Office for Northern Ireland   www.groni.gov.uk
General Register Office for Ireland   www.groireland.ie

Religious ceremonies

Church of England and Wales   www.cofe.anglican.org
Church of Scotland   www.churchofscotland.org.uk
Church of Ireland   www.ireland.anglican.org
Catholic Church   www.catholic-church.org.uk
Baptist Union   www.baptist.org.uk
Jewish Marriage Council   www.jmc-uk.org
Methodist Church   www.methodist.org.uk
Religious Society of Friends (Quakers)   www.quaker.org.uk
United Reformed Church   www.urc.org.uk

Interfaith advice

2-in-2-1   www.2-in-2-1.co.uk
Inter Faith Marriage Network   www.interfaithmarriage.org.uk

Name changing

UK Deed Poll Service   www.ukdps.co.uk
UK Identity and Passport Service   www.ukpa.gov.uk
Irish Deed Poll (Courts Service)   www.courts.ie
Irish Passport Service (Department of Foreign Affairs)
www.foreignaffairs.gov.ie

Local and national wedding suppliers

The Wedding Network   www.theweddingnetwork.co.uk
WeddingGuideUK   www.weddingguideuk.com
The Wedding Guide   www.theweddingguide.co.uk

Wedding shows

The Designer Wedding Show   www.designerweddingshow.co.uk
National Wedding Show   www.nationalweddingshow.co.uk
UK Wedding Shows   www.theukweddingshows.co.uk

Engagement and wedding rings

British Jewellers' Association   www.bja.org.uk
De Beers   www.debeers.com.
Lance James Jewellery   www.lancejames.co.uk

Outfit hire

Hire Society   www.hire-society.com
Moss Bros   www.mossbros.co.uk/hire

Stationery

Bride & Groom Wedding   www.brideandgroomdirect.co.uk
Special Day   www.specialdaydirect.co.uk
Wedding Stationery Gallery   www.wedding-stationery-gallery.co.uk

Stag and hen night parties

Big Weekends   www.bigweekends.com
Hen Heaven   www.henheaven.co.uk
Last Night of Freedom   www.lastnightoffreedom.co.uk
Party Box   www.partybox.co.uk
Your Vegas Wedding   www.yourvegaswedding.co.uk
Stag Weekends   www.stagweekends.co.uk
Stagweb   www.stagweb.com

Gift lists

Debenhams   www.debenhamsweddings.com
John Lewis   www.johnlewisgiftlist.com
Marks & Spencer   www.marksandspencer.com/giftregistry
Marriage Gift List   www.marriagegiftlist.com
Smart Wedding Lists   www.smartweddinglists.com
The Wedding Shop   www.weddingshop.com
Wrap It   www.wrapit.co.uk

Photography & Video

Association of Professional Videomakers   www.apv.org.uk
The Master Photographers Association   www.thempa.com
Society of Wedding & Portrait Photographers   www.swpp.co.uk
Wedding Photojournalist Association   www.wpja.org

Wedding insurance

E&L Insurance   www.eandl.co.uk
Events Insurance   www.events-insurance.co.uk
Wedding Insurance   www.weddinginsurance.co.uk
Wedding Plan   www.weddingplaninsurance.co.uk

Entertainers

EntsWeb Directory   www.entsweb.co.uk
Function Junction   www.functionjunction.co.uk
The Events Company.co.uk   www.theeventscompany.co.uk

Dance classes

First Dance UK   www.firstdance.co.uk
First Wedding Dance   www.firstweddingdance.co.uk
Dance Matrix   www.dancematrix.com

Sources for speeches

Famous Quotes   www.famousquotes.me.uk
Quotez   www.quotations.co.uk
Comedy Zone   www.comedy-zone.net

INDEX

AUTHOR'S ACKNOWLEDGEMENTS

The year 2006 has been an amazing period for both myself and The Wedding Network. In addition to co-presenting a BBC1 wedding show, I have been given the opportunity to write my first book, *The Groom's Guide,* which has been a fantastic experience. I have to say that it has been a team effort from all listed below, but I could not have done it without some help from friends in the wedding industry, so a big thank you to all. I would also like to thank:

Jacinda Love, my wife, for without your help this book would never have been written. You are my inspiration and my best friend; thank you for all your help.

The team at The Wedding Network, for all your help with research and content as well as putting up with me during the many weeks spent writing this book. Thank you once again for all your support.

To Lance at **Lance James Jewellery** (www.lancejames.co.uk), you are one of my best friends, and have spent many hours with me making sure of the accuracy and details of the engagement and wedding ring content of this book. I can only thank you once again for your endless knowledge in the jewellery business, and I cannot recommend a better jeweller to buy your wedding rings from.

To **Stag Web,** one of the leading stag and hen activities company, who kept me up to date on all the latest stag and hen destinations, as well as top tips to stay safe whilst travelling abroad. If you have not booked your stag or hen night yet, then check out the stag and hen section on www.theweddingnetwork.co.uk, or go to the www.stagweb.co.uk and quote TWN 101 to receive any special offers.

And to **New Holland Publishing.** When I first began penning this book, I was under the illusion that it would be quite an easy process, and written in no time at all, but boy, was I wrong. A massive thank you goes out to everyone at New Holland, as without them there would be no book in more ways than one.